Praise received for David Graves' work

"This workshop should be mandatory for all staff". *College lecturer*

"I'm a bully and I didn't know it! I would like to thank you David for opening my eyes, I leave here a reformed character". *Middle manager*

"Send my manager on this course". *Civil Servant*

"I now know I am not being bullied, just up against one of life's sad people, so I can get on with my life and not worry". *Civil Servant*

"Terrific stuff, great day! I am now going to implement an anti-bullying policy in my department". *Senior Manager, Local Authority*

"I have been bullied for two years and it has been devastating, this workshop has given me the confidence to do something about it, thank you". *Teacher*

"I hope all the senior staff are going ᵣ   .ᵣ ᴄourse". *Administrator, private industry*

"Every single person in this organisation needs this kind of training". *Local Authority employee*

"I never thought I had been bullied, I now realise that's why I was so unhappy in my last job, to be honest I thought I was useless and decided I had better leave before I was fired. Thanks David for putting it all to rest". *PA private industry*

"Brilliant day! Make it mandatory". *Civil Servant*

"Excellent! I especially liked the bit about what isn't bullying". *College support staff*

"David, have you ever thought about writing a book? It would be brilliant". *NHS employee*

"Until this workshop I thought it was just our industry that suffered bullying, now I know better". *Nurse*

Overcoming bullying
in the workplace

David Graves

THE McGRAW-HILL COMPANIES

London • Burr Ridge IL • New York • St Louis
San Francisco • Auckland • Bogotá • Caracas • Lisbon
Madrid • Mexico • Milan • Montreal • New Delhi • Panama
Paris • San Juan • São Paulo • Singapore • Sydney
Tokyo • Toronto

FIGHTING BACK: OVERCOMING BULLYING IN THE WORKPLACE
David Graves

0077099516

Published by McGraw-Hill Professional

Shoppenhangers Road
Maidenhead
Berkshire
SL6 2QL
Telephone: 44 (0) 1628 502 500
Fax: 44 (0) 1628 770 224
Website: www.mcgraw-hill.co.uk

British Library Cataloguing in Publication Data
A catalogue record for this book is available from the British Library

Library of Congress Cataloguing in Publication Data
The Library of Congress data for this book
is available from the Library of Congress

Sponsoring Editor: Elizabeth Robinson
Editorial Assistant: Sarah Butler
Business Marketing Manager: Elizabeth McKeever
Senior Production Manager: Max Elvey
Production Editor: Eleanor Hayes

Produced and typeset for McGraw-Hill by Gray Publishing, Tunbridge Wells
Text design by Robert Gray
Printed and bound in the UK by Creative Print and Design Group
Cover design by Senate Ltd

The publisher makes no representation, express or implied, with regard to
the accuracy of the information contained in this book and cannot accept
legal responsibility or liability for any errors or omissions that may be made.

Every effort has been made to ensure the accuracy of the information given
in this book at the time of publication, but it should not be regarded in any
way as a substitute for appropriate professional advice as and when
necessary. The author, David Graves, hereby disclaims any responsibility,
and will not accept any liability for any claim from any action based upon
any information given within this book.

McGraw-Hill books are available at special quantity discounts. Please contact the Corporate Sales Executive at the above address.

For Sylvie

My rock

Contents

Foreword

I am very pleased to have been asked to endorse this timely book which adds to our understanding of bullying at work and proposes ways of dealing with it.

Bullying at work is not a new phenomenon. It has existed in workplaces throughout the world for centuries. But, like so many other workplace issues – sexual and racial harassment, for example – it is only in recent years that it has been recognised for what it is, and policies and procedures have been devised to counter it.

I first became aware of, and interested in, the problem of bullying at work when I was a senior trade union official for the Manufacturing Science and Finance Union (now AMICUS). Bullying exists in public and private industry, in small and large companies, in the office and on the shop floor. And often it is part of a workplace ethos and culture. It is invidious, hard to prove, and difficult to stop.

Increasingly, however, employers are realising that bullying must be taken seriously and dealt with as soon as it is drawn to their attention, not least because of the cost of bullying and its effects on workplace relationships.

Attitudes are changing to bullying at work, and so is the interpretation of the law. Presently there is no particular law that covers bullying at work. I believe it would be a great step forward to introduce a piece of legislation designed specifically to outlaw bullying at work. That is why I have taken the Dignity At Work Bill through the House of Lords. However, until such a Bill becomes an Act, there are other actions that can be used to alleviate bullying.

This very perceptive book is both down to earth and extremely easy to read. Through its case histories it gives graphic illustrations of the kind of bullying that many workers have to face in their daily lives. It explores the basic effects of bullying – feelings of isolation, vulnerability and guilt. Many victims of bullying believe that they have somehow brought on the bullying themselves. They worry whether they are over-reacting or becoming paranoid, when the opposite is the truth. The book also defines what bullying is not – an understanding of this is especially important in order to get matters into perspective.

The chapters covering what triggers bullying and how to fight back, bullying and the laws and workers rights within the law are to be welcomed. It is of little use defining bullying without outlining the tools that can be used to counter it. Lastly, but not least, the book highlights the stress felt by those being bullied and its detrimental effects on them.

There is still much to be done to highlight bullying in the workplace. Anti-bullying polices and practices are increasing, but many more are needed. It is no good having written policies if they are not being translated into practice. All too often the victims of bullying believe that their only remedy is to leave their job. This book will be of tremendous help to those who are bravely standing up to bullying and to all those trying to find solutions to it.

Anne Gibson

Baroness Gibson of Market Rasen OBE

Preface

When I was first asked to write a book on workplace bullying, I wanted to do it in such a way that it could be read and referred to without readers getting bogged down with psychobabble and academic theories. The following is hopefully evidence of this. I decided to write from experience: not just mine but also the experience of others. While conducting my workshops on workplace bullying I have encountered hundreds of people who claim they have been or are being bullied; this book is intended to help them and the millions of others like them.

I want the book to be a toolbox from which you can draw the necessary tools to defend yourself against the bully and also fight back and beat the bully. I have both seen and experienced the personal devastation a bully can wreak. You may feel that devastation is too strong an expression to use; there are others: confusion, fear, self-loathing, panic and many more besides. If you are experiencing any of the above because of the culture in your workplace or the unwanted, undeserved personal negativity you are receiving from your boss or a colleague, then you are probably being bullied and this book will help you to fight back.

I have tried to include every possible type of workplace bullying, including examples of case histories to give you an idea of the many different ways that people can be bullied and the strategies you can use to fight back. Alongside this I have given you reasons for the bullying behaviour of the bully and how to combat it. At each stage there is a quick reference guide, something you can refer to once you have read the book without having to read whole sections again.

I am passionate about the need to eradicate bullying in all its forms. To do this it is essential that we all know what bullying is and know how bullies operate. We also need to be aware of some employers' role in passively encouraging bullying by their inactivity in the fight against it.

Bullying in the UK has reached almost epidemic proportions and is costing us dearly, not just financially but also in human terms. I would like to offer you a quote from Professor Cary Cooper of UMIST, our foremost expert on stress in the workplace, about bullying:

> The extent to which bullying goes on in British workplaces has reached phenomenal proportions. The damage can be irreparable, at worst causing suicide.

Not to put too fine a point on it, we all need to fight bullying wherever it rears its head. I will certainly continue to run my workshops and hopefully punch holes in the bullying culture wherever I find it. *You* can read this book and learn that you are not to blame if you are the target of bullying and begin to fight back!

Acknowledgements

I would like to thank the following people and organisations for their help and support during the writing of this book:

- Tim Field, founder of the UK National Workplace Bullying Advice Line for his unselfish sharing of information via his website Bully online (www.successunlimited.co.uk) and allowing me to dip in and out, cherry-picking information and reproducing figures.

- Professor Cary Cooper of UMIST for allowing me to quote him.

- UNISON for their permission to reproduce their survey on workplace bullying.

- Mike Appleby of Thompson's Solicitors for his painstaking efforts in trying to help a layman understand some very complicated law.

- Alex Mehta at freelawyer.co.uk for digging out some very relevant case law.

- Baroness Gould of Potternewton and Baroness Gibson of Market Rasen for all the information on The Dignity at Work Bill.

- Andy Ellis at www.workplacebullying.co.uk for allowing me to use his stress charts.

- Shrewsbury Industrial Tribunal office.

- Paul Scrivens for his encouragement and belief.

- Eric Plant, although cast away on foreign shores, he never fails to offer solid support.

- All my friends for their encouragement and genuine delight at this project.

- Sylvie and Carl for putting up with less attention (and the odd flash of temper!) while I locked myself away with this manuscript and yet still giving me their wholehearted support and encouragement.

If there is anybody that I have forgotten please forgive me and accept my heartfelt thanks for your contribution.

About the author

David Graves, an experienced facilitator of workplace bullying workshops, has been continually researching bullying in the workplace after becoming a target himself in 1995. Since 1996 he has run his own confidential consultancy and has delivered over 700 workshops, seminars and lectures on the subject, and spoken to hundreds of victims of workplace bullying. In the recent past he has been responsible for writing bullying and harassment policy for a number of organisations, at the same time as developing training programmes using popular TV drama to enhance the learning process and heighten awareness of the problem. David is also a director of Training To Go Ltd (TTG) and with permission from Pearson Television has developed a workshop about workplace bullying called 'Fair Play at Work', using an episode from the ever-popular TV drama 'The Bill'.

David can be contacted via e-mail at ttg@enta.co.uk

My own experience

When I was being bullied, I was not aware at first, what was happening to me. I really believed that I was at fault, that I was no good at what I was doing and was about to be sacked.

I would spend the morning drive into work worrying about what I might do wrong that day, and the evening drive home going through my day minute by minute and convincing myself that I really should look for another career, because I was obviously not very good at what I was doing. When I arrived home I would argue with my partner, not enjoy my food, mindlessly watch TV and go to bed exhausted, only to lie awake most of the night reliving my work day, yet again, and dreading the next one.

My contract with this organisation was a short-term contract but I had been assured that if it worked out I would gain a long term contract. My job involved working as part of a tight, interdependent team.

The undermining

Everything went well for the first couple of months. Then I discovered that unlike all the other team members I was not to be allowed to have a business card printed. I next discovered that I was receiving less in expense allowances than the others. The director who was instigating these attacks then issued a memo stating that I was not allowed my own telephone extension, would not be added to the telephone contact list and was not to be allowed specified desk space.

Permanency of employment?

While all this was going on the director concerned offered me (via the person who sponsored me to the company) the permanent contract I had hoped for. By now I was thoroughly confused by the mixed messages I was receiving. On the one hand it appeared that I was being consigned to the status of a nonvalued member of a team and on the other I was receiving an offer to become a permanent member of that team.

The day came when my contract was to be signed and I was summoned to the director's office. I arrived at her office in high excitement because I really needed the contract. Once seated I was told immediately that I was not to be offered a contract. Stunned, I asked why and was informed that the company was not offering any contracts at that time, although I knew that earlier that day two of my colleagues had been offered contracts. I had been led to believe right up to the eleventh hour that I was going to be offered that contract which everybody knew I needed so badly. This person who had been picking away at me for months, who then led me to believe that I was valued, at the last minute dealt me the cruellest of blows. I was devastated.

Even your family become victims

My family could not understand why this normally outgoing, confident person had gradually turned into a morose, bad-tempered, withdrawn shadow of his former self. I eventually sought help through my doctor and attended a stress management course.

It was during this course that the facilitator delivered a short module on bullying and it was like a lightbulb going on in my head. I now knew what had been happening to me and vowed to fight back. But even more, I decided to research the problem of bullying in the workplace and do something about it.

Lucky

However, I was fortunate and I was offered a contract with another company not long after, because if truth be told I really didn't have the strength to fight, nor was there any back-up in the form of company policy protecting staff against this form of attack. The other real truth is that, taken in isolation, each of the incidents that had happened to me seemed insignificant and even pathetic, or maybe even at a stretch could be put down to business needs decisions, but written down as a list they were a horrendous pattern of victimisation and a determined and deliberate undermining of one person by another.

Is it you they're after?

Subsequently, I discovered that I was not personally perceived as a threat to my tormentor but my sponsor was. This very good friend of mine was a popular, efficient and innovative member of staff. It was extremely difficult for my tormentor to get at him directly and because of this decided to 'pick off' those she could get at who held allegiance to him.

When we are targeted by a bully we always believe that in some way or another we are to blame; well, we are not! Throughout this book I will demonstrate how we can overcome this by fighting back.

Chapter 1

What is workplace bullying?

Where do all the bullies go?

As adults with responsibilities, jobs, bills, children to raise, etc., when we hear the expression 'bullying' we tend to relate it not to the world of grown-ups but more to the arena of the school-yard. Rarely do we ask ourselves the question, 'where do the bullies go when they leave school?' The obvious answer is they go to work. While accepting that not all will continue to bully as adults, we know that enough will, and along with those who don't start bullying until they become adults, cause havoc in the workplace.

However, knowing this is not enough, because in order to continue bullying people, the bully has to change tactics. As an adult in a work environment, thumping people, pulling pigtails, demanding chocolate biscuits or dinner money with menaces just isn't going to work. In the workplace the bully has to appear to be a different animal altogether in order that they may first subjugate and eliminate their targets.

In this book I want to explain what makes a workplace bully 'tick', how to recognise the workplace bully, the tactics he or she will use, what effect it is likely to have on the target, strategies to use to stop yourself becoming a victim and how to defend yourself if someone is trying to bully you, in other words I intend to give you the weapons to 'fight back'.

Defining bullying

Before we can fight back it is important to understand why bullies bully. To do this we have to look briefly at the psyche of the bully. First, it has to be recognised that anyone can be guilty of bullying behaviour. It's the easiest thing in the world to pick on somebody. However, most decent human beings stop when they realise the effect their unacceptable behaviour is having on the recipient and most will feel contrite. This can fall into the category of normal human behaviour. For example, we have all been guilty at one time or another of losing our temper or hurling abuse.

But the true bully can never be accused of a momentary behavioural glitch, the true bully knows exactly what they are doing and precisely how to go about it.

All bullying can be categorised as abuse

You would be forgiven for thinking that you would instantly be aware if someone was being abusive or you were being abused. The reason for this, of course, is that all of us know what the word abuse means, or we think we do. The problem we usually encounter occurs when we apply the norms to the word abuse:

■ violence
■ directed foul language
■ child abuse
■ sexual abuse

'Bullying is the unjust exercise of power of one individual over another by the use of means intended to humiliate, frighten, denigrate or injure the victim'.

Abuse

Oxford English Dictionary definition

'To insult verbally, the improper or incorrect use of power, insulting language, unjust or corrupt practice, mistreatment or assault of a person'.

Based on Latin *absus* 'misused'.

Here you can see that the definition of abuse could almost have been written to define bullying. The problem we have is that most workplace bullying is by stealth and we often cannot (unlike recognisable abuse) immediately see it.

- racial abuse
- power abuse
- position abuse.

As I said, these are easily recognisable forms of abuse, so recognisable that we rarely think beyond these categories.

What is the bully's problem?

So that you can begin to fight back effectively you have to know that the bully is weak. They look at their target and want whatever it is that they have got. But the bully is not prepared to admit they will never achieve this, or are too lazy or self-centred to bother. This is not a description of a strong, well-balanced person, it is the description of a person who is likely to be terrified inside and this can make them dangerous. They will often gather around them a group of easily led personalities among whom they can feel better about themselves.

Why do they bully?

You would be forgiven for asking the question 'why?' This question will be answered in great detail in other chapters, but for now it is worth pointing out that most targets of the bully are usually selected (and *selected* they are) because they are perceived as a threat, in some capacity, to the bully. It is also worth pointing out that the bully almost always chooses popular and efficient people to undermine. Again, this is usually because the bully suffers from low self-esteem that in turn leaves him or her feeling inadequate, threatened or jealous. Sometimes the bully subjugates people because their position allows them to and in order to lessen their own feelings of inadequacy. Being very good at your job is likely to uncover the bully's inefficiencies in their own job, whether the bully is a co-worker or a boss.

Bullies will also take advantage of those that they perceive as having a vulnerability that can be exploited, colleagues who need their jobs more than others, such as single parents, main bread-winners or even those who have recently suffered trauma such as divorce or bereavement.

Never forget that bullies only care about themselves. They need to feel better than the next person because they are genuinely unfinished human beings. They will target anyone they feel they can subjugate and, of course, while they are doing this they are deflecting attention from themselves and their own shortcomings.

The constituent elements of workplace bullying

When we examine workplace bullying we see offensive treatment by one person to another. This treatment is likely to be vindictive, malicious, humiliating and cruel. These attacks are persistently negative and aimed at both personal and professional performance.

They will almost always be irrational, usually unseen and often result in causing such chronic stress that a target can lose all belief in themselves, suffering physical ill-health and mental distress as a result. It is these elements that make up workplace bullying, the defining element being persistence. If the offensive behaviour is offered on a 'one-off' basis, unacceptable as it may be, we cannot define it as bullying. This is something I will refer to many times throughout the book.

Being able to describe or label what is happening to you is a way of making sense of what otherwise is a bewildering experience. As Andrea Adams once said, 'labelling this behaviour, "*bullying*", enables people to say I'm not imagining this – it is real, and it helps separate an entirely different set of experiences from, say, sexual or racial harassment'.

In future chapters I will differentiate between bullying and harassment; I will also look at the different types of bullying and harassment.

Quick reference guide 1

Reasons why some people are targeted

➡ They are perceived as a threat

➡ They are popular and efficient

Or, because the target:

➡ Needs to keep their job

➡ Is a single parent

➡ Needs to pay the mortgage

➡ Lives alone and has no one to give them support outside work

➡ Looks on the organisation and colleagues as an extended family

The target may be additionally vulnerable because:

➡ They have a different sexual orientation

➡ They are female in a male environment

➡ They are male in a female environment

➡ They have a different ethnic background

➡ Of their age – perceived as too young or too old

➡ They believe in doing their job properly

➡ They are recently divorced/separated/bereaved

Quick reference guide 2

The main elements of bullying behaviour

➡ Vindictiveness

➡ Maliciousness

➡ Humiliation

➡ Cruelty

➡ Negativity

➡ Irrationality

➡ Secretiveness

➡ Offensiveness

➡ Intimidation

➡ Persistence

➡ Jealousy

How bullying gets out of hand and ignored

So let's examine how workplace bullying can get out of hand, and why it escalates in a bullying culture. We also need to examine the consequences of this repeated, health-endangering mistreatment of a person by a cruel perpetrator.

It is best understood through the bully's behaviour, which can be categorised in the following way:

■ acts of commission which often reveal themselves as hostile verbal or non-verbal communication and interfering actions

■ acts of omission such as the withholding of resources, time, information, training, support and equipment.

Both are designed to guarantee failure or negate success and are driven by the bully's need to control the target. This usually involves the bully alone, in the first instance, deciding who is targeted, also when, where and how psychological violence will be inflicted. Later, others may be coerced, or even volunteer, to participate in the assaults.

If managers are involved this is not 'tough' or 'macho' management; it is (as is all bullying and harassment) illegitimate and often illegal behaviour, totally unrelated to accomplishing productive work, and so outrageous as to undermine the work itself.

There is a very real possibility of escalation from one-to-one bullying after it is reported and the employer responds inappropriately and inadequately. When an employee makes a complaint of bullying or harassment, it is at this point that it should be stopped. However, out of ignorance, fear or a mindset focused solely on profit margins and productivity (and sometimes malice), the complaint-takers in HR and lower-level management often choose to send the complainant back with one or more of the following messages:

■ That doesn't happen here, it is your imagination.

■ It's just a 'personality clash', work it out among yourselves.

■ Bitchiness is not illegal, what do you expect me to do?

■ Just toughen up, why are you so thin-skinned?

■ We all know how she/he is, it's her/his personality, learn to live with it.

■ Would you like to take a stress management course?

■ You need to understand the pressure she/he is under!

■ She/he is your boss, you'll have to live with it!

■ I employed/promoted her/him to 'sort out this team' and I'm happy with his/her results.

■ If you have a problem with 'success' work somewhere else.

Or they will use other similar discounting or deflecting statements of denial that clearly assert the organisation's lack of responsibility to help resolve the situation. This behaviour is not only short-sighted, but in the long run is likely to be detrimental to the firm and its longevity.

Some potential costs to an employer

■ Productivity is lost.

■ There is a risk of legal action being taken.

■ Any respect/credibility/trust by staff in the adequacy of the internal complaints process is lost. Eventually, the bully operates without senior management ever learning about the trouble brewing in the trenches.

■ Any team-building investment is lost.

■ Loyalty from employees is lost.

One thing that you can be absolutely sure of is that if you are a target of a workplace bully you are in the company of many other decent people who are just trying to earn a living. But even though bullying is rife it doesn't mean you can't fight back and it doesn't mean you can't beat the bully.

You are not alone

If you are a target of bullying at work you need to be aware that you are not alone. In some quarters it is said that half of all employees have, at one time or another, been the target of a bully at work. To be frank, no-one really knows just how many people have been attacked in this way. The only thing *I* know for sure is that the problem is rife throughout the workplace and is on the increase. In later chapters we will explore this in depth and work on strategies to enable you to fight back.

To demonstrate just how widespread the problem is I have gathered together some figures and information on professions where bullying is particularly rife.

NHS Trusts

Research commissioned by Grampian University Hospitals NHS Trust and carried out by Lyn Quine found that undue pressure being put on staff was the biggest complaint, while the withholding of information was another issue which caused staff stress.

The Police Service

The Police Federation of England and Wales has stated that it 'recognises that bullying within the workplace exists within the police service and commits itself to highlighting its damaging effects on police officers and eradicating it from the service'.

The Post Office

Recent research conducted by Professor Cary L Cooper for UMIST named Royal Mail/Consignia, part of the UK Post Office, as the worst employer for workplace bullying.

The private sector

There are many examples of bullying and harassment in the private sector. Walford v Ford Motor Company 1998 is a prime example, and like most cases in the private sector never made it to the courtroom. It is much easier and cheaper for a highly profitable company to 'pay off' (often on the steps of the court) the person who has a legitimate complaint than to suffer all the attendant publicity and costs that a tribunal is likely to bring, as happened in this case. Ford also insisted on a gagging clause as part of the settlement.

UK National Bullying Advice Line

The following statistics were kindly supplied by the UK National Bullying Advice Line (www.successunlimited.com), set up in January 1996 to help and advise people who are being bullied or harassed at work. Enquiries to date total 5756, of which 5204 are cases of bullying.

Since the inception of the website in November 1997 there have been in excess of 500,000 hits. The following percentages, which are approximate, have been consistent since the advice line's inception. Statistics are for the period from 1 January 1996 to 31 December 2001.

It is believed these cases are just the tip of the iceberg (all figures are approximate).

■ 20% are teachers, lecturers and school administrative staff

■ 12% are health-care professionals, including nurses, paramedics, GPs, etc.

■ 10% are from social services and caring occupations, including care of the elderly and people with special needs

■ 6–8% are from the voluntary and non-profit sector, with small charities (social housing, disadvantaged children, special needs, etc.) featuring prominently (these have usually involved a female serial bully); this sector has shown the highest rate of increase in calls since 1998

■ 5% are civil servants not included in the above groups.

This pattern (teachers, nurses, social workers and the charity/not-for-profit/voluntary sector being the top four groups) is also appearing via e-mails received from the USA, Canada and Australia.

■ 65% of enquiries are from the public sector
■ 30% are from the private sector
■ 5% are from students, retired people, etc.

About 90% of cases involve a manager bullying a subordinate; 8% are peer-to-peer bullying, and 2% subordinate(s) bullying their manager. The suspected true figures for peer to peer and subordinate on manager are likely to be higher, given that there have been few enquiries from factory and shop-floor environments.

Approximately 75% of callers are female, probably because females are more likely to be willing to admit they are being bullied, and more likely to be motivated to do something about it. Over 50% of reported bullies are female, probably due to the fact that teaching, nursing and social work have a higher than average percentage of female managers. The percentage of female bullies seems to be on the increase; however, bullying is *not* a gender issue. There are no hard data on bully–target gender combinations, but my impression is that a bully prefers a same-sex target on the basis that one knows one's own gender better (especially their weak spots) and, being intelligent, bullies are keen to remain outside the provisions of the Sex Discrimination Act.

■ 90% of enquiries involve a serial bully
■ 90% involve professional or office-based employees
■ 5% involve voluntary workers, students, etc.
■ 5% are manual or shop-floor workers.

About 5% involve probable racial, sexual or disability abuse or discrimination (this is a low figure because discrimination and harassment are well catered for by the Equal Opportunities Commission and Commission for Racial Equality and in UK law).

- 10% of cases involve contemplated suicide (it is suspected that the real number is much higher)
- 1% of cases involve attempted suicide (ditto)
- 12 cases involve actual suicide (ditto)
- 20% have taken, are considering or are taking legal action via an Employment Tribunal (this number has increased from 1998 onwards).

Knowing you are not on your own if you are targeted should help you to realise that the problem is not you. Once you realise that you are not to blame for what's happening to you, the confidence you need to begin to fight back will return. So let's examine how deeply rooted the problem is.

The workplace can be a dangerous place

If the figures on bullying at work are to be believed then the workplace can be a dangerous place to be in, not just for those who are targeted and victimised but also for their colleagues who suffer the extra workload and staff shortages brought about by the absenteeism and long-term illness that bullying causes. In turn this can lead to stress and higher levels of sickness among those who are not being bullied. So, I would argue that it is essential for all of us in the workplace to do what we can to stop workplace bullying wherever and whenever we see it happening. The following information on the cost of bullying in the UK was kindly supplied by Tim Field at www.successunlimited.co.uk.

The typical cost of bullying

Few employers understand how a bully impairs productivity, hinders performance and damages profitability. Let's look at a typical example of the effect of one serial bully on one department's performance.

- Population of the UK: **60,000,000**.
- Number of workers/employees: **28,000,000**.
- The majority of cases involve a manager bullying a subordinate in a professional or semi-professional context. The average wage for a subordinate lower–middle level manager or professional is around £20,000 a year.
- The effect of bullying on a targeted subordinate is reckoned to cut their work rate and effectiveness by **50%** (at least). Therefore, the annual cost of bullying is £10,000.
- The serial bully impairs the effectiveness of other employees, so say a further four employees earning £15,000 per annum have their performance impaired by **33%** (4 × £5000), plus a further eight employees earning £10,000 per annum have their effectiveness cut by **20%**, i.e. 8 × £2000 = £16,000.

Target: £10,000
+ 4 × £5000:   £20,000
+ 8 × £2000:   £16,000
                     £46,000

- *Experience from over 4000 cases suggests that these estimates are conservative.*

- The majority of bullying is carried out by a superior, so say the bully is a grade higher on a salary of £25,000 per annum. The serial bully is a dead weight so his or her annual cost is £25,000. Although glib and plausible, only when the serial bully leaves will it be discovered how little work that person completed: and much of that will be to a poor standard.

Serial bully: £25,000
Effect on employees: £46,000
                                  £71,000

- The lowest estimate of bullying, according to an Institute of Personnel & Development survey, was 1 in 8 workers bullied, which equates to around 3.5 million people. For safety, take an estimate of 1 person in 100 being a serial bully, therefore 1/100 of 28 million is 280,000 (less than 1/10 of the Institute of Personnel & Development's estimate)

280,000 × £71,000 = £19.88 billion

Cost of stress and stress-related illness (TUC, HSE, CBI, etc.): **£12 billion.**

Cost to UK: £38 billion per year.

This doesn't include consequential costs, legal costs, insurance costs, compensation costs, staff turnover costs, re-recruitment and retraining costs, loss of investment in training and experience, loss of employee potential, benefit costs, injury to health, loss of revenue due to employee being out of work and no longer paying tax, family breakdown, costs to society, etc.

UNISON survey

Below are some of the results of a survey commissioned by UNISON, carried out by Staffordshire University and Business School and sent out to 5000 randomly selected members of the union.

- ■ Two-thirds of members have either experienced or witnessed bullying.
- ■ 14% of members are being bullied in any six-month period, and for 34% of this group the bullying is likely to have gone on for three years or more.
- ■ 84.3% of currently bullied respondents state that the bully has done this before, and of those 73.4% stated that management knew about it.
- ■ 11% of bullied people reported they were bullied as individuals. For 32% of bullied respondents the whole of their working group was being bullied.
- ■ Most people are bullied by one person (63%). The most likely attribute of the bully is that they are a manager (83%).

■ For those who witness bullying, few (16%) have no reaction; most people experience stress (73%), while very few said their work improved as a result of witnessing the bullying (13%).

■ 92% of the respondents thought that bullying was caused by overwork.

■ 95% thought that bullying occurred because workers were too scared to report it, and 94% because the bullies could get away with it.

■ 26.4% of people who had been bullied previous to this survey reported they had left their jobs because of bullying.

■ Making a group complaint has the most negative consequences, with 96% of people doing this being threatened with dismissal.

■ Anger, stress and powerlessness are the most common reactions to being persistently treated in a negative way.

■ While confronting the bully was the most popular response for the currently bullied, it was effective in only 13% of cases; being labelled (43%) and even being threatened with dismissal (19%) were more common than managing to stop the bullying (13%).

■ Three-quarters (75.6%) of those who were being bullied reported some damage to their health. Stress, depression and lowered self-confidence were the most common non-physical complaints.

Other survey results

Date of survey	Survey origin	Ratio of employees bullied	Percentage workforce	Number of employees bullied (millions)	Period of bullying
Nov. 1996	IPD	1 : 8	12	3.5	5 years
Oct. 1998	TUC	1 : 6	18	4.5	1 year
Feb. 2000	UMIST	1 : 4	25	7.0	5 years
Jan. 1999	Lyn Quine	1 : 3	38	10.0	1 year
Jun. 1994	SUBS	1 : 2	53	14.0	Working life

Source: Andy Ellis, www.workplacebullying.co.uk

I think it would be fair to say that with statistics such as these, those of many other surveys and the reports we see almost on a daily basis in the newspapers and on TV, there is enough evidence to suggest that those of us who are being targeted or are actual victims of workplace bullying are not alone and the problem cannot be ignored.

If you need more evidence of this, or indeed need to seek support in any way, it may be a good idea to access some of the websites mentioned at the end of the book. But first you need to determine whether or not you are being bullied.

Chapter 2

Am I being bullied or just paranoid?

While it was relatively easy to recognise when we were being bullied at school, it becomes extremely difficult to recognise it when we are at work because of the subtlety that is used. It is also difficult, as an adult, to accept that we may be being bullied – because of the childhood connotations surrounding the word, it seems almost too foolish and weak to contemplate as an adult. But believe me, those who have suffered at the hands of the bully know only too well that tremendous strength is needed to combat them.

I have already mentioned many of the reasons bullies bully and make no apologies for reiterating that they suffer low self-esteem, they find it difficult to hold down relationships, they have difficulty in communicating effectively and are very jealous of people who are popular, have stable relationships and get on well with others. However, bullies are also often frightened of the people they bully, not frightened in the conventional sense of being scared of someone or something, but frightened of being exposed for what they are, and that is, not very good at their job.

Who is likely to bully you?

We have all met the supervisor, colleague or manager who we know should not hold the position that they do because, quite frankly, they are not up to it. If, however, you are good at your job the likelihood of their work being compared unfavourably to yours is a constant risk they are not prepared to take, so they begin to plot to remove you from the scene.

The colleague

There are many ways that they try do this. In the case of colleagues, for example, they will constantly and unjustifiably criticise your performance behind your back to other colleagues. They may even hint now and again to your manager that all is not as it seems with you. Remember, the bully is clever and will be well aware that criticising another colleague without good cause can easily backfire, so they will probably couch any criticism in light-hearted banter, then if anyone should question their remarks they can pass it off as a joke. All this is intended to focus other people's attention on you and keep people from noticing how inefficient they themselves are.

The manager

With a supervisor or manager the attacks are the same, but often the bully doesn't try to disguise them. They will probably perceive you as direct competition for their position and will persistently and unjustifiably 'nit-pick' your work, order all or part of it to be re-done, mock your efforts both privately and publicly, censure you by memo or e-mail and give unjustified verbal or written warnings. They may pile the work on to you, and you alone, knowing full well it will be too much, they may set targets that they know cannot possibly be achieved and if it looks like you may achieve them, move the goal posts to ensure you do fail. You may find that important information is withheld from you while being distributed to others.

Make no mistake, if this is happening to you on a regular basis it is designed to get rid of you because you are perceived as a threat and the bully cannot cope with their own feelings of inadequacy. **Think about this**. If you were genuinely inefficient then you could legitimately be removed from your position, and a good manager would certainly ensure that you were.

People like these, in positions of power, can stop leave, deny training and block promotion. They can give you negative appraisals and deliberately award responsibility to others not so competent or as senior as you in order to put you down. They can remove responsibility for no other reason than to make you believe you no longer have the trust of management.

A good example of how a supervisor tries to hide their inadequacies by using tactics of demoralisation is shown in the following case history.

Case history 1 (the office manager)

The problems started for the office manager when her new boss (PA to the managing director) arrived.

The office manager had responsibility for stationery and therefore held the keys to the stationery store. When trying to open the door one day she found her keys would not fit. When she informed her line manager of this she was told the lock had been changed and she no longer had responsibility for stationery. You would think it would be simpler to inform the office manager of the changes and take the keys back: if your intention is to undermine and humiliate it isn't.

The same office manager organised her leave around that of her colleagues and staff and informed her boss that she intended to take leave in a particular month. She also stated that she couldn't give an exact date because she intended to try and get a late booking bargain (something that had always been acceptable for all staff in the past). That weekend she found and paid for a holiday starting 14 days later. On the Monday she informed her line manager, who told her she couldn't have the leave because she (the line manager) needed six weeks' notice. This was contrary to company policy which stated only 12 days' notice was required. Although it was obvious that she would not be allowed to get away with this if the office manager insisted on taking her leave (which she did), the line manager had successfully started to make the office manager believe she had done something to earn disfavour.

When you add to this that the office junior was allowed the previous month to take annual leave at two days' notice, a pattern of malevolent behaviour directed at one person began to emerge. Eventually, after a number of other equally disturbing incidents directed at the office manager by the line manager, the office manager complained to her personnel department, the line manager was reprimanded and the bullying stopped.

But let's examine some of the reasons why this particular line manager would behave in this way to the office manager.

- The office manager had been with the company since its inception in the UK (the parent company was French), some seven years. Her line manager was new.
- The office manager could speak French, whereas her line manager could not.
- The office manager's line manager was personal assistant to the MD and had never before held a position at that level. She was not having a particularly easy time establishing a good relationship with the MD.
- The office manager knew most of the staff by name and was on first-name terms with the MD, who was also her department head.

■ The MD from time to time continued to enlist the help of the office manager to deal with sensitive tasks as he had often done in the past. It appeared that his PA felt that these tasks fell within her domain as she often quizzed the office manager about them.

So on the one hand, you have a long-serving, popular, trusted employee who was good at her job and possessed a special skill (an extra language). On the other hand you have a new employee with power who knows no-one, and is having difficulty dealing with her work and establishing a good working relationship with her boss. This is the perfect mix of unknowing target and frightened bully; frightened, that is, of being found out.

A good, experienced manager, or even a sensible person with little or no management experience, would use the experience and expertise of her or his staff to help them find their feet in a new organisation rather than subjugate those they felt threatened by. Deciding to undermine the nearest threat rather than developing good working relationships is almost rule one of the bully's code.

Other methods of subordinate bullying

Let's look at some of the other ways a manager/supervisor can bully you. We are all well aware of the old adage 'knowledge is power', and the bad manager, the insecure manager or the bullying manager is also aware of this and uses it to great advantage. By not passing on essential work-related information to staff, subordinates constantly have to refer to their manager for help and guidance. This in turn makes the manager appear to be more efficient than they are, staff appear less efficient and the manager comes across to those higher up to be 'hands on' and in touch with what's going on in the department. Of course, the bullying/inefficient manager will also use this to his or her advantage when things go wrong, saying: 'what can you do with

Quick reference guide 3

Some typical bullying behaviour

➡ Constant trivial criticisms

➡ False allegations of poor performance

➡ Setting tasks that they know are beyond a person's capabilities

➡ Excluding people from what is happening

➡ Whenever they are questioned they demand a 'meeting' to discuss the matter

➡ Issuing unwarranted verbal or written warnings

➡ Putting someone down in front of others regularly

➡ Denying leave for hospital appointments or on compassionate grounds

➡ Last-minute cancellation of holiday leave

➡ Compulsively and continuously lying

➡ Acting out of self-interest only

➡ Regularly hiding behind the employer: 'it's not me, it's the company' staff like mine? I have to constantly hold their hands and repeat instructions'. This is the type of manager who bullies all to hide their inefficiencies.

Are you seen as a threat?

The other type of manager/bully is the one that targets those they perceive as a direct threat to their position. They will ensure that all other staff will receive the information they require, but the person they perceive as most likely to show up their inefficiencies is the person from whom they withhold essential information. This person then has to ask for information on a regular basis in order to complete their work and gives the bully the opportunity to make comments along the lines of 'why don't you know this? Everyone else seems to.'

There is another form of bullying that needs to be mentioned here, '*the queen bee*' bully. This bully can also be male, not just female as the sobriquet suggests. They can also be either managers or colleagues and it doesn't matter if they have any real power or not, they still behave as though all *should* be subordinate to them. This bully has usually worked for the company for a long time and has gathered around them a group of sycophants who are greatly influenced by him or her. These queen bees decide whether or not you are acceptable to the group and if any member of the group tries to go against him or her then they in turn may become outcast.

Their power base often lies in their history. People may well have witnessed the ruthless speed and efficiency with which the queen bee has disposed of people in the past, and have decided it is better to side with them than try to go up against them. The bullying takes the form of the whole group getting involved in isolating an individual, not passing on information, excluding them from office socialising, such as birthday celebrations, leaving collections, and so on. This form of bullying can even go as far as sabotaging another person's work. The really clever aspect of this type of bullying is this that the queen bee rarely seems to be an obvious participant in the bullying behaviour. They seem to be able to influence and exert pressure on others to do the dirty work for them. In some cases they even pretend to befriend the target, but be sure it is they who are making the bullets for others to fire, and also be sure that in some way they will always let the target know of the influence they have over the others.

How basic workplace bullying manifests itself

Basic out-and-out bullying (or 'straight' bullying) at work is rarely physical and is, in the main, psychological. Anyone will do and it is difficult for anyone to spot the reason for the bullying.

When targeting an individual the bully is not looking for a level playing field: they do not want a fair fight. In this respect it's exactly the same as schoolyard bullying in that the target usually is weaker. Where it differs is that in most workplace situations the target is initially perceived as stronger or a threat in some way, and the bully actually weakens the target by subtly attacking them, often in ways that are not even recognised in the first instance as attacks.

The target may find that they are being stared at by their boss, on a regular basis, which in itself may not be thought of as being particularly offensive, but it can be intimidating. It may be that the target's views are never listened to, or suddenly the target is not invited to meetings they would normally attend. There are many different subtle ways in which the bully can weaken a target.

Why would anyone be treated in this way?'It seems that all a target has to do is meet the criteria of being popular, efficient and unsuspecting. What the bully does is bully for no reason other than assuaging their own fears, feelings of inadequacy and jealousy.

Quick reference guide 4

Bullying by no other name

➡ Bullying is almost always psychological and stealthy

➡ Anyone will do, especially if they are popular, competent or are perceived as a threat by the bully

➡ Bullying is always many incidents, often quite small, but when monitored display a pattern

➡ A victim often doesn't realise what is happening until it's too late

➡ The bullying takes place at work

➡ The bullying is a tool to control the threat of exposure

➡ The bully wants to control, subjugate and eliminate

Harassment

Some people believe that harassment is totally different from bullying, others that bullying and harassment are exactly the same. The truth is they are both one and the same but they *manifest* themselves in different ways. Unlike 'straight' bullying, harassment is not subtle. Harassment is obvious and you, the target, are left in no doubt that you have been selected.

How does harassment manifest itself?

Harassment usually has a 'hook' on which to hang the bullying. For example, it often has a physical element to it: contact or touch in all its forms or tends to focus more on the victim because of what they are, female or male, black, gay, disabled, because they are overweight or underweight, because of their religion or even because they are perceived as being a 'company' man or woman. Whatever it may be, it is because of this the harasser has their 'hook' on which to hang their bullying or harassment.

There are many laws in the UK and Europe that help people who are being harassed for specific reasons: the sexual harassment laws are a good example and I will detail them in a later chapter. But one of the laws which could have been be used to help the target in my next case history is The Protection from Harassment Act 1997, a relatively new act that provides individuals with recourse to the courts if they have been harassed on two or more occasions.

Case history 2 (Phillip)

Phillip worked for a large public employer and when I met him had been in position for about 12 months. He was a personable, smiley, overweight character considered by his employers to be a model employee. If given a task they knew he would perform it to the letter, and better still he would not take shortcuts or break any rules.

Phillip's job involved driving a van to various locations around the city at various times of the day and night and performing duties at these locations. Sometimes he was alone, at other times he had a 'mate' to accompany him, and on other occasions Phillip was the 'mate'. Most of the employees in Phillip's department were happy to work with him, even though they considered Phillip to be a little over fussy.

Like all the other employees Phillip was required from time to time to work overtime which, like the others, he was happy to do. In fact, there was often strong competition for the overtime work.

At the time Phillip joined the company had decided to implement new contracts which meant working a five, as opposed to four, day week (the same amount of hours) with less overtime. The job did not pay a particularly good salary and while benefits and job security were good, the overtime was almost a necessity. The employer was aware of this and the new shift pattern was also intended to share out the available overtime a little more fairly and save money by cutting the amount of overtime overall.

Disquiet in the ranks

Almost immediately a number of the 'old hands' became agitated by the changes and decided to oppose them. The employees that were making most noise were those that had enjoyed exceptionally generous overtime, in a number of cases as much as their salary again.

It was decided by a group of these dissatisfied employees that they would embark on a pattern of disruption which included among other things not working overtime. All this was unofficial and the union refused to support the action, but the agitators quietly went about their plans anyway.

Loyalty and standing your ground

Phillip, having started on the new contract and taken employment on this basis, believed there was no reason for him to become involved. This turned out to be the biggest mistake he had ever made in his life.

Phillip was approached on a number of occasions and 'told' he would regret not toeing the unofficial line. Phillip did nothing about these approaches; he just carried on fulfilling his contract, working hard and receiving more overtime than usual because others were not taking it. Here, I need to point out that Phillip was not alone: there were a few others who had started on the new contract. These others also continued to work in the same way as Phillip.

How Phillip was targeted

After a few weeks Phillip started to receive threatening phone calls at home. This time Phillip did report what was happening to his managers. Within 24 hours everyone in the department knew what was happening and the phone calls stopped. What happened next was a shock to everyone. Phillip started to receive letters (one of which is reproduced in Figure 2.1). These letters were not written or typed, but were constructed using words cut from newspapers and magazines. The letters made reference to Phillip's weight and were particularly obscene. The reproduction here is one of the milder letters.

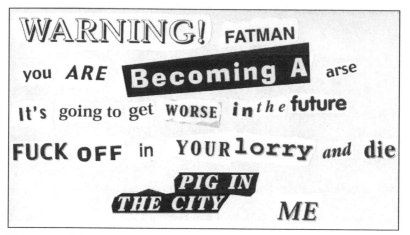

Figure 2.1 A facsimile of the letter sent to Philip.

Why Phillip was targeted

Phillip's workmates were not targeted in the way he was, and we need to understand why Phillip was chosen and not the others in order that we can better understand where bullying harassers come from.

■ Phillip stood out because he was obviously well liked by management.
■ Phillip had a weight problem.
■ Phillip got on with almost everyone.
■ Phillip was good at what he did.
■ Phillip complied with his contract.

The two points here that set Phillip apart from the others who were working in the new way, and gave his tormentors their hooks, were Phillip's weight and his popularity with management.

Why is this harassment and not 'straight' bullying?

■ There were 'hooks': Phillip's overweight and popularity with his managers.

Quick reference guide 5

Harassment

➡ Harassment tends to focus on the victim because of what they are – disabled, gay, black, female, etc. (the hooks)

➡ It is usually linked to prejudice, sex, discrimination, etc.

➡ You know you are being harassed straight away usually because of the offensive 'hook' language used, e.g. paki, poof, bitch, etc., or

➡ You have been physically assaulted, sexually assaulted or indecently assaulted

➡ Harassment is about domination and feeling superior

➡ Harassment often moves outside the workplace as well

➡ Often harassment can be for peer approval or bravado, etc.

➡ The harasser often lacks self-discipline

➡ The harasser often has specific inadequacies (e.g. sexual)

Because harassment is demonstrated in the way I have described the target knows immediately they are being harassed.

- The harasser's behaviour, although anonymous, was open and obvious.
- The harasser ensured that Phillip knew he was a target from the beginning.
- The bullying was taken outside the workplace.
- There was a great danger (implicit in the threats) of actual violence.

Remember, 'straight' bullying is almost always by stealth and is about undermining the target without them usually understanding what's happening until it's too late. There is no obvious 'hook' and it rarely moves outside the workplace.

Sadly, the culprit or culprits were never discovered. The police were called but could find no evidence that pointed them to a perpetrator. A series of bullying/harassment workshops was given to all staff, but bullying still goes on even though the management are doing everything in their power to stamp it out.

It is fair to say that managers had their suspicions as to who was harassing Phillip. A number of long-serving employees left within weeks of attending the workshops and no further instances of this type of harassment have occurred since.

So, are you being bullied or are you paranoid?'

If the type of behaviour I have detailed in this chapter is being directed at you on a regular basis, and here I must stress that bullying is persistent, then, yes, you are being bullied. If, however, you are suffering the odd incident of unacceptable behaviour then this has to be taken as a part of everyday working life, and you have to accept that not everyone you meet is particularly pleasant or helpful and deal with it accordingly. If, however, you are being harassed as I have described, and this happens twice or more, then, as I stated earlier, you are protected in law under The Protection from Harassment Act 1997.

What needs to be said at this point is that bullying rears its ugly head in many different guises and you can be targeted from a number of sources. But you must never lose sight of the fact that the bully is weak (even if they hold a position of power) because they are full of self-doubt and low self-esteem. You are in fact the stronger in this relationship because the bully fears you and provided you have the knowledge, and follow the advice given here, you will defeat the bully.

Chapter 3

What isn't bullying and different types of bullying

What bullying is not

If I am to arm you with the information required to fight back it would be remiss of me not to inform you of what isn't bullying. I know that while I was suffering the after-effects of being bullied I tended to overreact in certain situations. I felt that almost any negative comment was directed at me, and it did take a while to understand that even if the negativity *was* intended for me, I wasn't necessarily being singled out for special treatment.

I have mentioned before that not everybody we meet or work with is likely to be a decent human being, and from time to time we should expect to encounter conflict or even downright nastiness. But if we start crying 'Bully! Bully!' each time this happens, we are likely to gain a reputation as either a troublemaker, a whinger or a lunatic, or even be accused of bullying ourselves for making unsubstantiated and unjustified accusations.

Banter

Banter is usually carried out among a group or team of colleagues (in small organisations it may be the whole workforce) and often involves light-heartedly mocking each other or putting each other down. It sometimes involves language and figures of speech that may not be considered acceptable elsewhere in the organisation and it has the effect of helping a group or team feel close and special. Banter is often a generally accepted part of a work environment. It can help to make the day go more quickly and the workplace more bearable.

Banter can get out of hand

While not aiming to be a killjoy, banter can often get out of hand and end up doing the opposite of its intention which is to create a happy, productive workplace. You have to decide what is and isn't acceptable as banter: it's not just enough for you to know what you will or will not get involved in, you also need to find out what is acceptable to all the individuals involved. Banter in itself is not bullying, but if it moves into the area of constantly picking on something about somebody that they find hurtful, then you have to accept that it is their right not to have it happen to them, and you and/or the group must stop. If you don't stop then there is no doubt you will be guilty of bullying them.

Overhearing banter

It is worth remembering that banter that may not be offensive to one individual or group may very well offend someone over-hearing it. Even though remarks may not be intended for them they have a right not to have to put up with it.

- Always ensure remarks you make do not offend.
- Always ensure that people **not** involved in the banter are not likely to be offended.
- Racist remarks are never acceptable.
- Sexual touching is never acceptable.
- Bigotry is never acceptable.

Quick reference guide 6

What bullying is not

➡ An occasionally raised voice

➡ Legitimate and fair criticism of an employee's work

➡ Legitimate and fair criticism of an employee's behaviour at work

➡ Proper and correct monitoring of an employee under published company policy or because of suspected criminal behaviour

➡ An occasional argument

➡ Changing targets to suit business needs

➡ From time to time negotiating extra workloads to suit business needs

➡ Acceptable banter

■ Homophobic remarks are never acceptable.

■ Joking about people's disabilities is never acceptable.

Other types of workplace bullying

At this point I would like to offer brief descriptions (most of which are kindly supplied by Bully Online) of other types of workplace bullying that are known to exist and that we are able to define.

Corporate bullying

Corporate bullying is where the employer abuses employees knowing that the law is weak and jobs are scarce. For example:

■ Forcing employees to work overlong hours on a regular basis, then making life uncomfortable for those who object.

■ Dismissing anyone who looks like having a stress breakdown as it's cheaper (in the UK) to pay the costs of unfair dismissal at an Employment Tribunal (e.g. £50,000 maximum, but awards are usually much less than this) than risk facing a personal injury claim for stress breakdown (e.g. £175,000 as in the John Walker case).

■ Regularly snooping and spying on employees, e.g. by listening to telephone conversations without the employee's knowledge, conducting covert video surveillance, sending personnel staff to an employee's home to interrogate or photograph employees while on sick leave.

■ Not recognising work-related stress illness as anything to do with them and deeming any employee suffering from stress to be weak and inadequate. Refusing to accept that workplace bullying may be a related issue.

■ 'Encouraging' employees to give up full-time permanent positions in favour of short-term contracts; anyone who resists has their working life made uncomfortable.

Client bullying

Client bullying is where employees are bullied by those they serve. For example, teachers are bullied (and often assaulted) by pupils and their parents, nurses are bullied by patients and their relatives, social workers are bullied by their clients, and shop, bank, building society and Benefits Agency staff are bullied by customers. Often the client is claiming their perceived right (to better service) in an abusive, derogatory and often physically violent manner. Client bullying can also be employees bullying their clients.

Serial bullying

Serial bullying is where the source of all dysfunction can be traced to one individual, who picks on one employee after another and destroys them. This is the most common type of bullying I come across; this person exhibits the behavioural characteristics of a socialised psychopath. Most people know at least one person in their life with the profile of the serial bully; most people do not recognise this person as a socialised psychopath, or sociopath. It is estimated one person in 30 is either a physically violent psychopath who commits criminal acts, or a person whose behaviour is antisocial, or a sociopath who commits mostly non-arrestable offences.

Residual bullying

Residual bullying is the bullying of all kinds that continues after the serial bully has left. Like recruits like and like promotes like, therefore the serial bully bequeaths a dysfunctional environment to those who are left. This can last for years.

Secondary bullying

This is mostly unwitting bullying that people start exhibiting when there's a serial bully in the department. The pressure of trying to deal with a dysfunctional, divisive and aggressive serial bully causes everyone's behaviour to decline.

Pair bullying

Pair bullying is a serial bully with a colleague. Often one does the talking, while the other watches and listens. It's the quiet one you usually need to watch. Often they are of opposite gender and frequently there's an affair going on.

Gang bullying (in Europe known as mobbing)

This is a serial bully with colleagues. Gangs flourish in corporate bullying climates (unlike the queen bee who usually create their own bullying micro-climate). If the bully is an extrovert, they are likely to be leading from the front and may even be a shouter and screamer, thus becoming easily identifiable (and recordable on tape and video).

If the bully is an introvert, that person will be in the background initiating the mayhem, but probably not taking an active part, and may thus be harder to identify. A common tactic of this type of bully is to tell everybody a different story – usually about what others are alleged to have said about that person – and encourage each person to think they are the only one with the correct story. Introvert bullies are the most dangerous bullies.

Half the people in the gang are happy for the opportunity to behave badly; they gain gratification from the feeling of power and control, and enjoy the patronage, protection and reward from the serial bully. The other half of the gang is coerced into joining in, usually through fear of being the next target if they don't. If anything backfires, one of these coercers will be the scapegoat on whom enraged targets will be encouraged to vent their anger.

The serial bully watches from a safe distance. Serial bullies gain a great deal of gratification from encouraging and watching the conflict; especially those who might otherwise pool negative information about them.

Gang bullying or group bullying is often called mobbing and usually involves scape goating and victimisation. This form of bullying is often prevalent in factory environments and the construction industry.

Vicarious bullying

Vicarious bullying is where two parties are encouraged to engage in adversarial interaction or conflict. It is similar to gang bullying, although the bully may or may not be directly connected with either of the two parties. One party becomes the bully's instrument of harassment and is deceived and manipulated into bullying the other party. An example of vicarious bullying is where the serial bully creates conflict between employer and employee, participating occasionally to stoke the conflict, but rarely taking an active part in the conflict themselves.

Regulation bullying

This is where a serial bully forces their target to comply with rules, regulations, procedures or laws regardless of their appropriateness, applicability or necessity.

Cyber bullying

The misuse of e-mail systems or Internet forums, etc., for sending aggressive flame mails is cyber bullying. Serial bullies have few communication skills (often none), and so the impersonal nature of e-mail makes it an ideal tool for causing conflict.

Quick reference guide 7

Flaming

What is 'flaming'?

The inappropriate use of e-mail to:

➡ Make racist/sexist remarks

➡ Send pornographic material

➡ Undermine another person

➡ Censure another person

➡ Make derogatory comments about a person

➡ Gain political capital over another

➡ Send persistent negative memos

How to deal with 'flaming'

➡ Do not reply in kind (this may escalate the behaviour)

➡ Do not delete the e-mails

➡ Make a hard copy

➡ Let the appropriate people in your organisation know what's happening

The figures below taken from a NOP survey commissioned by Surfcontrol plc, document the depth of the problem.

In London 55% of employees polled use email as a political tool to highlight a colleague's mistake in front of others, in Manchester this was 34% and Edinburgh 32%. In London 36% of employees polled send racist, sexist, pornographic and discriminatory emails, in Manchester this was 36% and Edinburgh 28%.

Bullying by e-mail is, on the one hand, very disturbing the language used is often very direct and bruising. However, it can also be reassuring because it is easy to gather evidence against the bully as everything is documented, and the source is obvious.

Quick reference guide 8

Bullying traits

➡ Bullies never admit to being wrong

➡ Bullies blame others, never themselves

➡ Bullies are insecure

➡ Bullies find it difficult to hold down steady relationships

➡ Bullies get angry easily

➡ Bullies are jealous of other people's success

➡ Bullies take credit for other people's work

➡ Bullies are often charming to people they need to impress or keep in with

➡ Bullies remember only what they want to

➡ Bullies are good at twisting the truth

➡ Bullies are devious and often dishonest

➡ Bullies need to control others and events

➡ Bullies are vindictive

➡ Bullies suffer from low self-esteem

➡ Bullies don't trust others

➡ Bullies pick on people in front of others

➡ Bullies hold back information

➡ Bullies refuse reasonable requests

➡ Bullies don't listen to other people's points of view

Quick reference guide 9

Is this happening to me?

➡ Am I being publicly humiliated?

➡ Am I receiving constant unjustified criticism?

➡ Am I being excluded?

➡ Is my work being sabotaged?

➡ Am I having responsibility taken away for no good reason?

➡ Am I being censured by memo or e-mail?

➡ Are my efforts being constantly undervalued?

➡ Are my applications for leave being blocked?

➡ Am I unjustly being passed over for promotion?

➡ Am I stopped from attending training courses?

➡ Am I receiving an unfair and impossible workload?

➡ Am I receiving unjustified verbal or written warnings?

➡ Has my workspace been gradually eroded?

➡ Are my targets always changing just as I get near to achieving them?

➡ Are my reasonable requests for new equipment constantly being turned down while others aren't?

➡ Is work-related information not being given to me?

➡ Am I having to comply with rules that do not conform to company policy?

➡ Am I suffering groundless withdrawing of privileges, such as my car parking space, my office, my own telephone extension or business cards?

Because bullying is subtle and underhand the target often doesn't realise it until it is too late.

Third-party bullying

This is when the bully is trying to undermine somebody they perceive as a threat but cannot directly bully them. Instead, they bully those closest to the person they are trying to undermine, thus whittling away the target's supporters.

You are not to blame

If you are a victim or target of bullying the most important thing to remember is that **you are not to blame**. No matter what you feel about yourself, no matter if you feel your age may be against you, be you young or old, no matter if you are male or female, you can guarantee that the bully will be targeting you because they are jealous and frightened.

They are jealous because you are efficient, because you are popular, because you can communicate with others, and because your relationships seem in good repair. They are frightened because your efficiency shows up their inefficiency, because they can't relate to men, or to women, and if they are your boss they may be frightened that you will usurp their position.

When bullies target people in the workplace what they are doing is attempting to project their own inadequacies onto their victims. Most people are bullied because they possess the qualities the bully most desires for themselves. Because of this the bully is determined to eradicate their chosen victim, and if you start to believe that what is happening to you is all your fault, eradicate you they will.

So let us look at some of the questions you need to ask yourself.

Am I good at what I do?

I suggest the first question you need to address is: are you good at your job? Each of us is aware of our level of competence, but when defending against the bully you need to be brutally honest with yourself and ask yourself whether the reason someone is questioning your abilities is justified or not. If you are content that your ability to do your job should go unquestioned then you have to look for reasons why someone should be suggesting that you are incompetent.

So let us examine how you do your job. If, for example, you find it easy to work without supervision, tend to grasp what's needed quickly and get on with it, then others in your team may resent this because they cannot perform in this way. They may need constant supervision or they may often miss the point of what is expected of them and need to refer to their manager on a more regular basis. Maybe your manager has asked others why they can't be more like you and held you up as the example to be followed. While praise for the work we do is always welcome, and essentially we all crave it and often work harder for it, it has to be accepted that not everyone on the team can be expected to enjoy seeing others praised.

Many years ago, I was a trainer for a company selling home improvements direct to the public. It was my responsibility to train the salespeople. Each month sales teams from all over the country would gather in one place to receive praise and motivational talks. Each month the same few individuals were held up as shining examples of how the work ethic, combined with good skills, equalled achievement. Following this came the motivational 'talks' during which those perceived as non-achievers were subjected to the 'why can't you be like these high achievers?' spiel. This was considered to be motivational, but often had a negative effect, causing some people to leave and others to induce disruption within teams, in some cases falsifying orders to make themselves look better, and causing some truly vitriolic nastiness toward those who achieved from the underachievers.

It is fair to say that in some cases all this had exactly the desired effect and spurred people on to achieve more.

What has to be accepted here is that the sales environment is a naturally competitive one, and people working in this environment expect to receive a fairly vigorous 'motivating' from time to time. Yet it still engendered petty jealousies and abuses of the achievers by the underachievers.

Competitiveness

I am not suggesting that a competitive environment is wrong or that employee-of-the-month competitions, for example, are a bad thing. Quite the contrary, I believe that these types of initiative are terrific motivators but they can set up some recipients of these ovations as targets. If you have an inefficient work colleague who may already see you as possibly showing them up, receiving a public accolade for your work is as good as putting a target on your back saying 'bully me'. Furthermore, although bullying can occur in environments that are highly competitive you have to be more alert in less competitive environments.

If, as we said earlier, you work well on your own, use your initiative and are not in need of constant supervision, you may find that you are perceived by your manager or supervisor as a threat to their job.

Good managers, bad managers

A good manager will be glad to have staff that work in the way that you do, but an inefficient or insecure manager will always worry that you will eventually show up the deficiencies in his or her work. Also, if you are this self-motivated you will have less need to seek help and advice from your manager who, lacking in self-esteem, may become paranoid about this, which may lead to your being bullied by your manager.

If you are popular with other members of staff, have a solid relationship at home and appear at ease while communicating with others, you may be targeted by those who do not have the ability to enhance their own lives in this way. Conversely, it may be that you are self-contained and, while friendly and helpful, don't go in for soul baring, small talk or out-of-work activities, such as lunches, pub crawls, coach trips and so on. Again, this may encourage someone who is looking to deflect attention from their own inadequacies to target you for bullying.

Dressing up or down?

Something as basic as being well dressed may be the catalyst for abusive behaviour towards you. I have worked in environments where there has been no dress code and in these environments staff often opt for the lowest common denominator: jeans and T-shirt. I have witnessed well-dressed members of staff being treated badly by others just because of this; having comments directed at them like, 'I bet he's gay', 'How can she afford to dress like that?', 'Her boyfriend must be rich' or 'Look at that, dressed up like a dog's dinner just for work'.

It may seem that what I am saying is, anything that separates you from the crowd is likely to attract bullies to targeting you, and I am saying just that. I am saying this in order to make you aware that you could be targeted just because of other people's petty jealousies and inadequacies.

- Am I saying change? No!
- Am I saying you're to blame? No!
- Am I saying become paranoid? No!
- Am I saying be aware? Yes!
- Am I saying develop strategies to fight back? Yes!

But what I really hope you will take away from this chapter is this: just because you are good at what you do, just because your personal life is OK, just because you find it easy to get on with people, just because you like to dress smartly or even just because you don't conform to others' perceptions of the norm, this does not entitle others to pick on you. No-one has to put up with being bullied, everyone has the right to go to work and not be made to feel miserable. If this is happening to you because of the reasons spelt out here then in order that you can start to fight back, you must make a conscious decision **not to take the blame!**

If, when you look at the list in Quick reference guide 10 you can truthfully say it applies to you, even in part, if you are aware that you are being targeted by a bully, and if you are prepared to accept that you are not to blame, then you have to make a decision. You either get out and find another job which, if there is no support for you where you are, may be the only option, or you stay where you are and fight back. Whichever option you choose is the beginning of your regaining some of the confidence that you may have lost because of the bully's actions against you.

Quick reference guide 10

Why you are NOT to blame!

➡ You are competent at your job

➡ You get on with others

➡ You don't put others down

➡ You are honest

➡ You have integrity

➡ You are loyal to your company

➡ You believe in a fair day's work for a fair day's pay

You are not responsible for:

➡ The inadequacies of others

➡ Other people's low self-esteem

➡ Other people's jealousies

➡ Other people's dishonesty

➡ The inability of others to accept responsibility for their own lack of ability

➡ Your organisation employing people who are not up to the job

➡ Your organisation promoting people who should never have been promoted

➡ Your organisation not training managers in effective people management

Chapter 4

Fighting back

A bully is not only likely to pick a target for the reasons given in previous chapters, but there are certain events that are likely to trigger bullying behaviour and the bully is likely to strike after one of the following events, so you need to be on your guard.

Events that can trigger bullying behaviour

Bullying often starts after one of these scenarios:

- The previous target leaves.
- There's a reorganisation.
- A new manager is appointed.
- You may have unwittingly become the focus of attention whereas before the bully was the centre of attention (this often occurs with female bullies): most bullies are emotionally immature and thus crave attention.
- Obvious displays of affection, respect or trust from co-workers invoke the bully's jealousy.
- You refuse to obey an order which violates rules, regulations or procedures, or is illegal.

■ You stand up for a colleague who is being bullied: this almost always ensures that you will be next; sometimes the bully drops their current target and turns their attention to you immediately.

■ You blow the whistle on incompetence, malpractice, fraud, illegality, breaches of procedure, breaches of Health and Safety regulations, etc.

■ You undertake trade union duties.

■ You challenge the *status quo*, especially unwittingly.

■ You gain recognition for your achievements, e.g. winning an award or being publicly recognised.

■ You get promotion.

As I have already said, it is after events such as these that you need to be intensely aware that you may be targeted. This is the time that you are most vulnerable to attack. The obvious tactic here is to ensure that you are never affected by, or involved in, any of the above, but you will be well aware that this would be impossible. You would have to become a hermit, withdrawing completely from any form of social or workplace intercourse and forget any ambition you may have, but none of this need even be considered if you behave assertively.

Assertive behaviour

I have mentioned many times that the bully is a coward and he or she is likely to shy away from confrontation (except, of course, the shouting and screaming extrovert bully). I suggest that one of the most effective ways of not allowing the bullying to start in the first place is to employ assertive behaviour: not just with anyone you feel may bully you, but with everyone. Make assertiveness part of your personality, work on it, until it becomes second nature for you to deal with everyone in an assertive manner.

Assertiveness can, if used properly, stop the bully in his or her tracks, by letting the bully (and everyone else you deal with) know that:

- you will not be pushed around
- you can say no
- you are prepared to stand up for your rights
- you can and will respond only to reasonableness.

The basic philosophy of assertiveness

Assertiveness is standing up for your rights in such a way that you do not violate another person's rights. It means expressing your wants, needs, opinions, feelings and beliefs in direct honest and appropriate ways.

Assertiveness is **not** aggression: aggression is about getting your own way at the expense of others, putting them down, manipulating them, or making them feel incompetent, worthless or stupid; in short, bullying them.

Assertiveness is **not** passive: passivity means you ignore your own interests and goals. It means waiting for others to initiate activity and ideas.

Assertiveness is **not** about avoiding conflict: it is about handling conflict openly and directly and coming to a workable compromise, providing that compromise does not violate your own feelings of self-worth.

Assertiveness is based on the following beliefs

- You have needs to be met.
- The other people involved also have needs to be met.
- You have rights, so have others.
- You have a contribution to make, so have others.

If you behave in this way people will learn that you, while being reasonable and helpful, will not be pushed around and it will send out a strong signal to bullies that it would be best to leave you alone.

Consider your rights assertively

■ You have the right to be treated with respect as an intelligent, capable and equal person.

■ You have the right to state your own needs and set your own priorities as a person independent of any roles you may assume in your life.

■ You have the right to express your feelings.

■ You have the right to express your opinions and values.

■ You have the right to say no or yes for yourself

■ You have the right to make mistakes.

■ You have the right to change your mind.

■ You have the right to say 'I don't understand' and ask for more information.

■ You have the right to ask for what you want.

■ You have the right to decline responsibility for other people's problems.

■ You have the right to deal with others without being dependent on them.

Assertiveness is about respecting yourself, defending your right to be yourself and taking responsibility for yourself. For example, 'I feel angry when you put me down' is more assertive than, 'you make me feel angry when you put me down'. It is no bad thing, when considering a request for which you have no immediate response, to ask for 'thinking it over' time.

When you are behaving assertively you have to allow for the fact that you will make mistakes and accept it; in fact, you should be giving yourself permission to make mistakes. If you are prepared to do this it will allow you to combat the bully who falsely accuses you and you won't immediately be intimidated (as people often are) by the thought of making a mistake. This will give you the time you need to realise you are not making the mistakes the bully claims, and allow you to formulate your strategy for fighting back.

Fighting aggression assertively

Because most bullying is psychological in nature, the aggression used is a secondary or low-level type of aggression (this does not mean it is any less humiliating than shouting or screaming). The bully will often use sarcasm: 'this is indeed a masterpiece', or the bully may try patronising an experienced member of staff as a means of putting them down: 'you will let me know if it's too difficult for you, won't you?' Deliberately not listening or not letting you voice your opinion is another bullying tactic and example of this type of aggression.

Responding assertively is essential in these circumstances. Often our immediate reaction is anger: 'who do they think they are?' This means the bully is achieving his or her objective, to undermine you. If, however, we possess sound, unflustered, assertive thinking, our thoughts are more likely to be along the lines of 'I have made a mistake, that's OK, I can fix it' or 'if it's too difficult for me I will certainly ask for help'. Because bullying behaviour often comes at you from the left field it's vital that your assertive head be on at all times so that you are certain of what the bully is saying and why they are saying it.

Good, sound assertive thinking will enable you to ask calm, unhurried questions: 'what is wrong with it?' or 'would you like to run it by me first?' Behaving like this can diffuse the attack and may even put the bully off targeting you. Remember, you have given yourself permission to make mistakes and you know you are good at your job.

Quick reference guide 11

Assertive statements

'I' statements that are brief, clear and to the point

➡ 'I prefer'

➡ 'I feel'

➡ 'I think'

➡ 'I don't think that is true'

➡ 'I can't accept that'

Distinction between fact and opinion

➡ 'My experience is different'

➡ 'I know this to be true'

➡ 'I know that to be false'

Useful phrases for saying No!

➡ 'I feel uncomfortable saying it, but, no'

➡ 'I'm saying no this time but please ask me again'

➡ 'I should have said this weeks ago, but, no'

Phrases that allow you thinking time

➡ 'I see'

➡ 'Let me see'

➡ 'Well'

➡ 'Fine; let me think about it'

Defending yourself

Of course, being assertive does not guarantee that you will not be targeted, nothing can do that. So if the bully has breached your defences let's examine some other ways to fight back.

Again, the first thing you have to do is be aware. If you believe you fit the criteria for becoming a target then you will possess a certain amount of self-confidence and self-awareness. This, of course, can lead you into believing you are safe, so it will come as a shock when you realise you are being targeted.

This, in turn, can lead to self-doubt and self-blame. You must not let this happen! A defence strategy has to be implemented. Once you have established that you are being unfairly criticised or receiving unfair workloads or you are being sidelined you have to have an action plan.

Making a case

Because of the bully's deceitfulness and because the bully's preferred methods rarely include witnesses (except in the case of gang bullies, see page 40) you have to rely on your own record of events. It is essential that you make a note of every incident, including dates, places, times and the names of any witnesses. It is worthwhile pointing out that making a note of how the incident made you feel can sometimes be a very important factor in helping someone else to understand how bad the problem is.

Confronting the bully

Confronting the bully is a daunting task for anyone, but it can be done and done effectively if you plan the confrontation and do it on your own terms. As with any plan it has its downside as well as its upside.

The downside of confrontation

■ The bully will know you are on to them.

■ The bully will try to escalate the argument.

■ The bully will disclaim any knowledge of what you're talking about.

■ The bully will try to blame you.

■ The bully may threaten and try to intimidate you.

■ The bully will not show fear.

■ The bully will lie.

The upside of confrontation

■ The bully will know you are on to them.

■ It will frighten the bully.

■ The bully will know you have gathered evidence and witnesses.

■ You will feel better about yourself.

■ You will have saved your job.

■ The bully will know that you are prepared for a fight.

■ The bullying of you may stop at this point.

You may want to take a colleague into the meeting with you as the confrontation is likely to be behind closed doors and this will provide you with a witness.

It may be that, even accompanied by a friend or colleague, you would not want to confront the bully, but you must still talk to someone. There are a number of reasons for this. First, it will help you to understand better what it is you are facing if you vocalise it. Secondly, it will make you feel less alone, and finally, an independent objective view will help you to see whether you are overreacting or not. You could talk to:

■ a dedicated harassment officer (if the company has one)

■ your union representative

- a counsellor
- the Citizen's Advice Bureau
- a company welfare officer
- a company nurse
- a personnel officer
- your manager or the bully's manager
- a friend
- in dire circumstances, a lawyer.

Collecting evidence

Workplace bullying can be difficult to prove, but it can be done. Because it can cause severe health problems in the form of stress-related illnesses, some employers are reluctant to accept that it happens. The biggest fear that some employers seem to have is being sued, never mind that education of staff could help to eradicate bullying (and thus the fear of being sued), never mind that staff would be happier in a non-bullying environment, never mind that happier staff would be more productive and never mind that individuals and their families may suffer.

You and I *know* when we are being encouraged or fairly criticised and we also *know* when we are being treated unfairly, and when this happens it our responsibility to ensure that it is brought to the attention of our employer. It is also absolutely essential that we provide evidence of the bullying.

Persistence

You know that the bully is going to be persistent; they will not give up easily. This will give you plenty of opportunity to compile a list of incidents with dates, witnesses, times and how they made you feel. It is no use complaining of being bullied if you cannot back it up with some form of evidence. You might argue that it is only your word against theirs, but the question has to be asked: why would you bother if it weren't true? You must also remember that the bully will not be expecting this and will find it difficult to defend against because it demonstrates a pattern.

Feeling silly

It may be that when you are compiling your list you may feel that some of the incidents you are detailing are silly and inconsequential. I have to agree that taken in isolation some of the attacks a bully makes are silly and hardly worth bothering about, but when you have many small attacks that on their own would mean nothing, looked at altogether they form a pattern of persistent and pervasive undermining of one individual by another. Furthermore, you *will* become worn down by them and they *will* get to you.

Compiling a list of these incidents not only is another way of defending yourself against the bully, but can also be therapeutic in itself. It will help to stop you blaming yourself and give you the self-confidence to fight back.

Case history 3 (Joan)

An example of putting into action that which I have just described occurred with an experienced middle manager in the Civil Service.

Joan had worked for the Civil Service for 15 years and had a responsible role within her department, managing a team of 23 people. She was a confident, middle-aged woman who had earned the respect of colleagues and staff alike.

New manager

A new senior manager was transferred from another district and had overall responsibility for the district in which Joan worked. From the beginning Joan noticed he had a fondness for patronising people and jokingly putting them down in front of others. After a few weeks Joan realised that this behaviour appeared more and more to be directed at her. Joan mentioned to him that she felt that being patronised by her senior manager was inappropriate and asked him to stop, at which point the senior manager laughed and suggested that she display less emotion in the workplace. To accompany this he actually patted her on the shoulder before walking off. It didn't finish there, however: as he was walking away he passed one of Joan's staff and said 'steer clear of Joan, she's having a bad hair day'.

Joan's feelings

Can you imagine how this made Joan feel? She felt humiliated: here was a strong, 'together' woman who had just been put down in front of staff by her senior manager. To an onlooker, however, this whole incident may have been seen as light-hearted banter, until you examine the following points:

- This was not the first time something like this had happened.
- Joan had attempted to behave in an adult manner and been treated in a way that accorded her little respect for her position or her experience.
- Joan had attempted to broach a serious subject and it had been treated as a joke.
- If Joan were to try to explain this to an onlooker they might be forgiven for thinking Joan was overreacting.

The effect on Joan

It doesn't matter how this behaviour was intended, the effect it had on Joan was to make her believe that her senior manager was not likely to take her or her views seriously. This in turn started Joan wondering what she had done wrong. Of course, she had done nothing wrong, but each day Joan spent more and more time wondering when she was going to be attacked again. It didn't help that the senior manager was generally regarded as a bit of a charmer and even when Joan tentatively broached the subject with her deputy, the deputy said that she didn't think the senior manager's behaviour was anything other than good-natured banter. This put Joan into even more of a spin, not knowing whether or not she was overreacting or being oversensitive or had just simply lost her sense of humour. All these conflicting thoughts served to make Joan feel inadequate as a person and she began to lose confidence in her abilities.

What Joan did next

Joan decided that she had to fight back, but felt that because of the way others perceived the senior manager she had to gather some evidence of what she believed to be happening to her. There was no way that Joan could begin grievance proceedings because she believed (correctly) that without evidence she wouldn't be taken seriously.

Joan decided to keep a log of every incident, which contained:

■ details of each incident
■ names of witnesses
■ dates and times of incidents
■ where the incidents took place
■ how the incident made Joan feel

At the end of one month Joan had recorded 33 separate incidents where she believed she had been deliberately undermined by her senior manager. Staggeringly, this averaged out to over one and a half attacks per working day.

Confirmation

Even with all the evidence the log presented, Joan still wanted to confirm that she wasn't overreacting. Joan decided to phone her senior manager's previous office on the pretext of finding out the date of his birthday, with the hope that during the conversation she would gain some insight into how his previous staff had perceived him, and hoped this would confirm her own beliefs. She needn't have worried. The response to her request for the information was: 'you're not thinking of sending Mr Snidey a card are you? Blimey, he must have changed his spots!' It transpired that her senior manager had behaved in exactly the same way at his previous office and that the staff were overjoyed at his departure.

Confrontation

This was exactly what Joan needed: confirmation that she wasn't losing it. She made her mind up that the time had come to resolve the problem and rehearsed what she was going to say.

Joan decided that the best time to confront her tormentor was first thing in the morning. She gathered together all her notes, placed them in a file and set off for his office. Joan admits that she was terrified and that with each step she was becoming less and less confident, but she was determined; she knocked on his door and went in.

Joan began by stating that she believed she was being victimised, to which her senior manager immediately responded, 'oh Joan we're not getting all emotional again are we?' Joan says that at this point her legs were going and she felt sick, but was determined to see it through and she used this statement: 'I believe that for some reason you have deliberately tried to undermine me since you came here and I have no intention of allowing it to continue. I have gathered together all the evidence from each incident along with witness names, times and dates and if you don't stop immediately I'm going to instigate official grievance procedures against you.'

> Joan's manager asked to see her evidence. She declined, stating that if he didn't stop his insulting behaviour, which she believed to be bullying, towards her, he would be given the evidence before an official grievance hearing. Joan finished by stating that all her evidence would be placed in the care of her union representative but would remain sealed provided the bullying stopped. Joan refused to be drawn into further discussion of the matter, left his office, copied all the evidence and handed a sealed copy to her union rep for safe keeping.

The bully moved on

Joan has never had a problem with this bully's behaviour towards her since. She has, however, noticed that he behaves in the same unacceptable way to another member of staff. Unfortunately, Joan is still recovering from being bullied herself and feels that she doesn't have the strength to become involved on someone else's behalf just yet. However, she is compiling a dossier of incidents she has witnessed which she will hand to the current target when appropriate. In Joan's own words, 'why should one man be allowed to move from person to person causing them misery at work?'

At the time of writing this situation is still continuing and in all honesty probably will for some time to come. It is obvious that Joan and those before her and those since have all been the target of a serial bully (see page 39) who is causing misery to those around him with his dysfunctional behaviour.

For Joan the strategy she employed worked: it got the bully off her back. Others, however, may not be so lucky and they may very well find that their only option is to leave; but if you are targeted here is another strategy you could try.

The letter

If your bully has made unwarranted criticisms or false allegations about you, or has put you down in front of others or made demeaning remarks, how can you turn it to your advantage and reflect it back on the bully?

Record the criticism, allegation, remarks or behaviour in a letter to the bully. For example:

> On [*date*] you made the following criticism/allegation/ remark [*quote it exactly*] or behaved in an unacceptable manner [*describe the behaviour exactly*]. I now ask you to provide me, in writing, with substantive and quantifiable evidence to justify your criticism/allegation or provide me with good reason for your remark/behaviour.

You should state that not only do you expect a reply in writing, but it is the only kind of reply you will find acceptable. This will put the bully on warning that you are onto them:

■ Yes, it will generate a response.

■ Yes, it may force a confrontation.

■ Yes, it may turn ugly.

But:

■ It will get the problem out in the open.

■ It will help you to decide whether or not to make it official.

■ It will force the bully to make some choices.

■ It will make you feel better, because you are fighting back.

Points to remember

If the bully ignores your letter and continues to bully you, you have to decide whether or not to make it official or to write again asking for a reply. If the bully ignores your letter but stops bullying you, you have to make a decision whether or not to pursue it by insisting on a reply or dropping it. I suggest you drop it but remain on your guard. If the bully confronts you in an aggressive manner, walk away and make an official complaint. Do not get drawn into an argument.

If the bully is prepared to discuss the matter rationally, accept this and get the bully to agree not to continue with the unacceptable behaviour. It is a point worth making, that they may not be truly aware of what they are doing or the effect it is having on you.

It doesn't always work

It is a given that in a society that has no actual law against bullying it may be difficult to prove and sometimes targets don't get the result they want. But it isn't impossible, and many people do receive satisfaction, as I will demonstrate. There are many different laws that cover the behaviour which is often displayed when a bully is operating in the workplace, and some of these laws make some bullying behaviour criminal offences. I will cover these in a later chapter.

So why doesn't it always happen that fighting back can give you the result you need against the workplace bully?

- It may be that the culture of the organisation is founded on bullying behaviour.
- It may be that the bully is perceived as being 'too valuable' to lose.
- It may be that you just can't prove it.
- It may be that you are simply not believed.

The stages of fighting back

If you're a bully's target, what else can you do? First, report it. If it's a co-worker, go to your boss. If it's your boss, move up the

Quick reference guide 13

How to defend yourself against the bully

➡ Make a note of every incident

➡ Take the names of any witnesses

➡ Write down how the incident made you feel

➡ Talk it over with a colleague, your boss or a friend

➡ If you can, calmly confront the bully and tell them how their behaviour makes you feel and tell them they should stop

➡ If confronting the bully is difficult for you alone then take someone with you, not to join in but just to be there

➡ Speak to your union if you have one

➡ Write a letter

➡ Speak to a counsellor

➡ Take advice from the Citizen's Advice Bureau

➡ Speak to the personnel department

➡ Institute grievance procedures

➡ Seek legal advice

management chain. And make it clear that it's not simply a misunderstanding or an interpersonal conflict. Even though bullying is not illegal under current workplace legislation, companies should move swiftly against it. Employers should take the bully behind closed doors and challenge them on their behaviour, making it clear that their job may be in jeopardy if it continues. It is not advisable to join your boss in conversation with the bully.

Traditional conflict resolution is based on rationality. Bullies are not rational. What they will do is sit in that meeting and lie. If you are there as well it is likely that heated argument will ensue. In fact, it's more than likely they will attend the meeting and suggest that they are the one being targeted, they've been picked on, or they've been discriminated against.

A company also can use practical, day-to-day business practices to deal with bullies. Your office should have an anti-bullying/harassment policy which should cover all forms of harassment, not just the illegal ones. If these remedies fail, an employer can usually make a valid case for the bullying employee's dismissal by documenting the behaviour, just as is done for a non-performing employee or one who commits an act of gross misconduct.

The bullying employer

Whatever the reason, if you cannot make people understand what has been happening to you, then you must consider looking elsewhere for work. This is unfair and wholly unreasonable, but in a way this is also fighting back because, as we have established, you are a loyal, efficient employee and as such are a valuable resource. So why not take these qualities where they will be appreciated more?

Leaving your job will cause the following problems for your employer. They will have to advertise for, train and allow settling in time for your replacement. All this will cost them money and

Quick reference guide 13

The stages of fighting back

➡ Speak to a friend or colleague

➡ Speak to your welfare officer

➡ Speak to your line manager

➡ If your manager is the bully, speak to their manager

➡ Speak to your union representative

➡ Speak to the personnel department

➡ Invoke company grievance procedures

➡ Seek advice from the Citizen's Advice Bureau

➡ Take proper legal advice

➡ As a last resort, seek satisfaction at an Industrial Tribunal at the end of it your replacement may not turn out to be suitable or may even leave because of receiving similar treatment to you.

Of course, you can always negate the need for any of this by checking out your employer before you apply to work for them. A bullying employer or company whose work culture either condones or at least does not inhibit bullying is reasonably easy to spot.

How to spot a bullying employer

You may be impressed by a company's vision or mission statements, or by impressive training or government certificates, and while in many cases these may be deserved, some quality and best practice awards can be used by unscrupulous employers to hide what's really going on. Ask around the area: a lot of information about employers can be gleaned from locals, shopkeepers, newspapers and the like. If possible, speak to current employees.

The sort of information you need

- rate of staff turnover
- number of early retirements
- number of suspensions
- number of dismissals
- number of times the employer is involved in Industrial Tribunals or legal action against employees
- are they generally believed to be a good employer?

Some of the language used when making enquiries or attending an interview may be another indicator that the ethos of the company may encourage or accept bullying behaviour.

Quick reference guide 14

Some language to help you recognise a bullying culture

➡ Strong or robust management

➡ Kicking ass

➡ Macho management

➡ Aggressive work ethic

➡ We run a tight ship

➡ We don't have people here who rock the boat

➡ We don't suffer fools gladly

➡ We *always* pull together

➡ Most of our managers are keen enough to take work home

➡ You will often find office lights on as late as nine o'clock at night

➡ I'm always the last to leave

➡ In the case of a woman – do you have plans for a family?

➡ In the case of a man – you don't believe in this paternity leave nonsense do you?

Quick reference guide 15

Pointers to help you recognise a company that has a bullying culture

➡ More managerial levels exist than are necessary

➡ Scapegoats are sought to blame for things that go wrong

➡ The absence of one person means that key decisions are not made

➡ People doing the same job are rewarded differently, and in a way that is seen to be unfair

➡ Influential senior managers are near to retirement and have no desire to rock the boat. As a result, change and those that try to create it are viewed as a potential threat, and their attempts at change are blocked or worse

➡ Confidence in the leadership does not exist

➡ Employees get little or no feedback on their performance

➡ Rumours abound

➡ Management style is command and control

Chapter 5

Bullying, the law and tribunals

No law against bullying

I have already mentioned that in the UK there are no laws specifically designed to combat workplace bullying. You have to identify the areas of law that are closest to what you are suffering and base your case on them. The MSF union (now AMICUS) proposed the Dignity At Work Bill to address these discrepancies.

It received its second hearing supported by Baroness Gould of Potternewton on 4 December 1996 in the House of Lords. Here are the first two paragraphs.

> My Lords, bullying, harassment and victimisation can take many forms. The list is endless but typically consists of unfair and excessive criticism, publicly insulting the victim, ignoring the victim's point of view, constantly changing or setting unrealistic work targets, withholding information in order to embarrass, undervaluing efforts, shouting and abusive behaviour. All of these this important Bill is attempting to eradicate.
>
> While we have protection against sexual or racial harassment, there are many people who have no such

protection because they fall into a gap in legislation to cover people who have complaints of this form of bullying.

The upcoming general election meant that this Bill did not progress any further. However, the Bill was reintroduced by Baroness Gibson of Market Rasen and has passed through the House of Lords unopposed after its third reading. In brief, the new Bill provides for the following:

Right to dignity at work

1. Every employee shall have the right to dignity at work and if the terms of the contract under which a person is employed do not include that right they shall be deemed to include it.

2. Subject to section 5 of this Act, an employer commits a breach of the right to dignity at work of an employee if that employee suffers during his employment with the employer harassment or bullying or any act, omission or conduct which causes him to be alarmed or distressed including but not limited to any of the following:

   a) behaviour on more than one occasion which is offensive, abusive, malicious, insulting or intimidating;

   b) unjustified criticism on more than one occasion;

   c) punishment imposed without reasonable justification; or

   d) changes in the duties or responsibilities of the employee to the employee's detriment without reasonable justification.

This Bill when it becomes law will give protection to a section of the workplace that at present has to piggyback on other legislation to seek redress. I would like to examine some of those laws and how we may use them in the rest of this chapter.

The right to be accompanied

In September 2000 new provisions under the Employment Rights Act 1999 came into force whereby workers have a right to be accompanied at disciplinary or grievance meetings. The person chosen to accompany you can only be a fellow worker or trade union representative or official, which is somewhat limiting. But even so it's never advisable to attend a disciplinary hearing on your own.

Employment Tribunals

Most workplace grievances will be dealt with at Employment Tribunals, a much cheaper route than going through the courts. It is also more informal and therefore less intimidating, but it is still advisable to seek professional help with presenting your case.

The procedure

It is imperative under employment law that the correct procedures are followed. You must in the first instance make any claim to an Employment Tribunal within 12 weeks of leaving your employment, or if you are still in employment, from the time of the offence or the unsatisfactory completion of internal disciplinary procedures. The court will not extend this period except in the most exceptional of circumstances. The following steps are **exactly** those required by the local Tribunal office when you wish to make an application for redress at Tribunal.

Steps to Tribunal

■ First, you must fill in form **IT1** which you can get from your local Tribunal office.

■ Next, return the form to the office and they will inform the employer and respond to you, usually within five days.

■ The next stage is usually a pre-tribunal hearing, the details of which should be given to you within 21 days, setting a date for a Tribunal, usually within the following six months.

■ At this point ACAS (who will also have received the applicant's submission and the employer's response) may decide to contact both parties and try to negotiate a satisfactory outcome prior to any Tribunal appearances.

■ If ACAS do not become involved or cannot resolve the situation, then the pre-tribunal hearing will go ahead to decide whether there is a case to answer.

■ If it is decided that there is a case to answer then a date will be set for a full Tribunal.

■ If the Tribunal decides that there is no case to answer then, in the normal course of events, that is the end of it. However, if the applicant decides that they still wish to continue they can, but they must first lodge a £500 deposit and be prepared, if they lose, to have costs awarded against them.

■ If it is decided that there is a case to answer and a Tribunal goes ahead no costs can be awarded to either party. Both parties have to pay for their own legal representation no matter what the outcome.

■ The decision of the Tribunal can be appealed (known as an Employment Appeals Tribunal or EAT); you can even take it to the House of Lords, but you have to fund all your legal representation and, again, be prepared to foot the bill for your opponent's legal costs if you lose.

Formal procedures at work

Tribunals place great emphasis on whether you have looked at every option open to you, especially, and including your employer's dispute procedures. If you have followed your employer's dispute procedures and they haven't given you satisfaction, or have broken down or proved inadequate, a Tribunal will look more favourably at your case than if you haven't followed these procedures at all. **The Tribunal may even reject your case on this point alone**.

So, even if your employer's procedures are wholly inadequate, a Tribunal will expect you to have attempted to seek satisfaction in this way. However, if your employer has no formal procedures in place, a Tribunal is likely to look unfavourably on the employer's defence.

> A study by Manchester School of Management in 1998 found that of 165 tribunal decisions, in every case where the employer had no formal procedures, the employer lost.

You must always remember that Tribunals will only make judgements under existing law; to do otherwise would mean a case being overturned on appeal.

Employment Rights (Resolution Act) 1998

This Act can be used for the resolution of tribunal cases without the need for a full tribunal hearing.

- *Determinations without a hearing or full hearing.* This is allowed where the case is uncontested or where the tribunal feels it doesn't have the jurisdiction to hear the case.
- *Hearings, etc., by chairman alone.* Allows for the carrying out of pre-hearing reviews by the chairman alone and the hearing and determination of preliminary issues where it involves hearing witnesses other than the parties or their representatives.
- *Hearings by chairman and one other member.* This is allowed in certain circumstances by the Act.

Quick reference guide 16

Steps to take when seeking satisfaction in law

➡ Ensure you have exhausted all company procedures

➡ Keep a diary of all events including names of witnesses, even reluctant ones

➡ Seek proper medical advice and treatment if you believe that the bullying you have received has made you ill

➡ Seek proper legal advice, ensuring your legal advisor is competent to deal with employment issues

➡ Ensure that your legal advisor understands what bullying is (give them this book to read)

➡ Fill in form IT1

➡ Ensure that you respond to all correspondence from the court

➡ Hand all correspondence from your employer to your legal representative

➡ Don't stop pestering your legal representative

➡ Keep up with everything that is going on

It is absolutely essential that the legal representative you retain knows what bullying is and that they are fully qualified in the area of employment law. You may want to access www.freelawyer.co.uk who can supply you with a list of competent practitioners.

Remember, you have 12 weeks in which to register for a Tribunal, six years in which to bring a breach of contract action and three years in which to start a personal injury action. These time limits are rigidly enforced.

Out-of-court settlements

It may be that before you get to court your employer offers a settlement. Before accepting any such settlement seek legal advice and remember that if a settlement is offered it is often a sign of guilt.

Negotiated settlement

Many applicants, if offered an out-of-court settlement, are asked to sign a gagging clause. The legality of such a clause is dubious. A gagging clause is usually inserted in any out-of-court settlement for two reasons: first, to ensure that you don't take further legal action against the company and secondly to ensure that you don't talk publicly about the case or circumstances leading to the case.

It may be worth remembering that if a settlement is being offered the chances are that the organisation that has abused you feels that you have a strong case. What you are being given here is another chance to fight back and you should negotiate the settlement rather than simply accepting what is first offered. For example, you may indeed agree to take no further legal action and also accept a gagging clause if the settlement offered is singnificantly increased. It is widely recognised as standard negotiating practice not to agree to anything without gaining something in return.

History

Another point worth remembering is that most bullying cases have a history behind them and no organisation wants a public airing of this history.

Employers who have protected a bully and failed to protect you really do want all this to be kept secret. Add to this the fact that you are likely to suffer the aftermath from having been bullied for a long time, so why should they get away cheaply?

Different laws

Let us examine the different laws that may help you to receive satisfaction (in the absence of bullying law) if you have been bullied. As I have already mentioned, the absence of redress in law for the bullied sometimes makes it difficult for the bullied to prove that they have indeed been wronged in this way.

Constructive dismissal

This is one of the nearest areas of law to which bullying can be allied. If the conduct of the employer was such that they left you no option other than to leave for the sake of your health and well-being, then this is the law to which you can turn. In order to claim constructive dismissal you must first have resigned your position.

One-year qualifying period

In 1999 the length of time for which you must have been con-tinuously employed by the same employer which would enable you to bring a claim for constructive or unfair dismissal was reduced from two years to one year. So, if you have not been continuously employed by the same employer for at least one year you have no case in law to make.

Upper limit

The current limit on compensation for unfair or constructive dismissal is £51,700. However, the compensation awarded in most cases of unfair or constructive dismissal is considerably less than this.

Employment Rights Act 1996

If you are in the process of being unfairly dismissed, and especially if your employer is not following the correct disciplinary procedures for dismissal, you may be able to apply for a High Court injunction to prevent the dismissal.

Breach of contract

The breach is of the implied term of mutual trust and confidence. Constructive or unfair dismissal itself constitutes a breach of the implied term of mutual trust and confidence. Every employee is entitled to a (written) contract of employment which states what both employer and employee expect of each other. The contract (even if it is not in writing) is valid only while both parties behave in a trustworthy manner: this is the 'implied term'. Bullying is a breach of this implied term of mutual trust and confidence.

In the case of Johnson v Unisys, Lord Steyn stated, 'It is no longer right to equate a contract of employment with commercial contracts. One possible way of describing a contract of employment in modern terms is as a relational contract.'

Health and Safety at Work Act 1974

This covers breach of duty of care, as well as the provision of systems of work that are, so far as is reasonably practicable, safe and without risks to health. The bully's behaviour constitutes a breach of the employer's duty of care under the Act because employers have a legal obligation to ensure both the physical and psychological well-being of their employees. The Act requires employers to provide both a safe *place* of work, and as far as is reasonably practical, a safe *system* of work. If, having brought a health and safety issue to the attention of the employer, the employer chooses not to take action, they will be in breach of this Act. In high-risk and high-stress environments, the employer may be legally obliged to carry out a risk assessment.

Vicarious liability

In a sense, vicarious liability is liability from a distance, in that an employer can be held liable for an employee's actions if those actions cause injury to himself, or indeed if he were to cause injury to another employee, and the employer knew or ought to have known the potential for such injury to occur and did nothing to prevent it.

Lister v Hesley Hall [2001] IRLR 60

This landmark House of Lords ruling clarifies the vicarious liability of employers for criminal or negligent acts of their employees. Basically, if the employer is deemed to have control over the 'unsafe' system then he may be liable and responsible both civilly and criminally.

Sex Discrimination Act 1975

This covers discrimination on the grounds of sex by dismissing an employee or submitting them to 'any other detriment'. If the bully and target are of different genders or different sexual orientation, it may be possible to claim sexual harassment or sexual discrimination. There are other clues to look out for when determining whether or not sex discrimination is taking place. For example, you might notice that all promotions or new jobs are being awarded to people of the same gender. As I have pointed out earlier in this book, bullying lies behind all forms of harassment and discrimination. Many harassers have inappropriate attitudes to sexual behaviour or may even have sexual problems.

Race Relations Act 1976

This is the same as the Sex Discrimination Act but covers inequality on racial grounds. If the bully and target have different skin colour or are of different racial, ethnic or cultural origin (which includes prejudices within the same country or language, for example English versus Welsh), it may be possible to claim racial harassment or racial discrimination. Remember that bullying is behind all forms of harassment and discrimination.

Disability Discrimination Act 1995

This covers discrimination on the grounds of disability or perceived disability. If the target of bullying has a recognised disability [anything in ICD-10 or DSM-IV (diagnostic codes) which a GP or consultant is prepared to put in writing] and this disability is known to the employer, if may be possible to bring a case under this Act. This includes 'stress and anxiety caused by work'. You can use this Act from the second day of employment

and you don't have to resign in order to start tribunal proceedings.

Trade Union Reform and Employment Rights Act 1993

This covers rights for blowing the whistle in health and safety cases, and carries with it the possibility of substantial compensation. Under this Act, if an employee reports a health and safety matter to their employer and is subsequently victimised for doing so, a tribunal is empowered (under the ERA s44) to award substantial compensation. In addition to health and safety matters, victimisation may be on the grounds of Sunday working, pension fund trustees or employee (union) representation. You can claim victimisation from day two of your employment (there is no qualifying period) and there are no limits on compensation.

Victimisation is where an employee suffers detriment; the word 'detriment' is not defined in the Employment Rights Act and as such can be interpreted widely. An employee is subjected to a detriment if he or she is put at a disadvantage. To prove disadvantage you will need to identify a comparison, which may be hypothetical or actual. If an employee is worse off (e.g. because of his or her position *vis-à-vis* health and safety, or union membership or non-membership) than a comparable fellow employee, then he or she is at a disadvantage and has thus suffered a detriment.

European Working Time Directive

This directive limits the working week to 48 hours. There are exceptions and employees can 'voluntarily' sign away their right to not have to work more than 48 hours per week. But being bullied into (by having the threat of redundancy or demotion

held over your head) working non-agreed longer hours, or being *expected* to take work home may constitute a breach of this directive.

Public Interest Disclosure Act 1998

Unfair dismissal or redundancy or detriment for blowing the whistle in the public interest is covered by this Act. A worker may take his employer to Tribunal for any detriment (dismissal, redundancy, etc.) after the worker makes a disclosure (i.e. blows the whistle) relating to any of the following:

- a criminal offence
- a breach of legal obligation (e.g. duty of care)
- where the health and safety of an employee is likely to be endangered (a good example is bullying)
- a miscarriage of justice
- environmental damage,

and where information is likely to be deliberately concealed, provided that the worker:

- reasonably believes it to be true
- does not make the disclosure for personal gain (e.g. leaking information to the press for money)
- does not commit an offence by making the disclosure (e.g. breaking the Official Secrets Act).

Criminal Justice and Public Order Act 1994

This covers intentional harassment causing another person alarm or distress by using threatening, abusive or insulting words or behaviour.

Protection from Harassment Act 1997

Both criminal and civil provisions are now in force covering harassment and stalking. This Act may be of use if the bully regularly harasses you or members of your family. It is becoming more and more unacceptable for a boss to phone you regularly at home, either to consult you on business matters (especially if they berate you) or while you are on sick leave or on annual leave, and especially if the calls are at unsocial hours.

Breach of confidentiality may be regarded as an act of harassment. The DTI recommend using the Protection from Harassment Act against bullies in the workplace (remember, two or more provable acts of harassment are enough to bring a case), although in reality the Act is designed to deal with stalkers.

Under the Protection from Harassment Act, it's the target's *perception* of the harassment rather than the perpetrator's alleged *intent* which is significant (e.g. if you inform someone that their behaviour towards you is unacceptable and they don't stop, they cannot at a later date claim they didn't intend their behaviour to be interpreted in a negative way). This is a first in UK law.

Negligence

Waters v London Metropolitan Police

After Waters v London Metropolitan Police (27 July 2000) it is now legally possible to sue for negligence for the psychiatric injury resulting from the employer's failure to protect employees from bullying, harassment and victimisation, remediable in damages for which the respondent is vicariously liable or for intimidation or for acts of misfeasance in a public office.

Here are some of the words used by Lord Slynn of Hadley in the Court of Appeal:

Two features of the claim need to be emphasised. In the
first place there is no allegation of a conspiracy between
the various police officers named to harm or to fail to
look after the appellant. In the second place the appellant
does not rely simply on individual acts taken separately;
she attaches importance to the cumulative effect of the
acts particularly in regard to the causation of psychiatric
injury which she alleges. In the appellant's case before
your Lordships some 89 allegations of hostile treatment
are listed as taken from the statement of claim. They are
summarised in the appellant's case as being repeated acts
of

'1. Ostracism including refusal or failures to support her
   whilst on duty and in emergency situations,

2. Being "advised" or told to leave the police force,

3. Harassment and victimisation, and

4. Repeated breaches of procedure.'

Some of these allegations taken alone may seem relatively
minor. Others are much more serious. There are,
moreover, complaints that more senior officers reporting
on her wrote unfair reports sometimes with the purpose
of pushing her out of, or persuading her to leave, the
police force. She says that she was excluded from duties
she could and should have carried out. Evans LJ in his
judgment in the Court of Appeal has summarised the
main events at the various police stations where she
served. I gratefully adopt and therefore do not repeat his
summary. At the heart of her claim lies the belief that the
other officers reviled her and failed to take care of her
because she had broken the team rules by complaining of
sexual acts by a fellow police officer.

The principal claim raised in the action is one of negligence:
the 'employer' failed to exercise due care to look after his
'employee'. Generically, many of the acts alleged can be seen
as a form of bullying: the 'employer' or those to whom he del-

egated the responsibilities for running his organisation should have taken steps to stop it, to protect the 'employee' from it. They failed to do so. They made unfair reports and they tried to force her to leave the police.

You will have noted his Lordship's use of phrases such as, 'the appellant does not rely simply on individual acts taken separately' and 'some of these allegations taken alone may seem relatively minor, she attaches importance to the cumulative effect of the acts particularly in regard to the causation of psychiatric injury which she alleges'. This only appears to underline what I believe to be the first line of defence and the first steps of fighting back. That is, keep a list of attacks, note any witnesses and write down how the attacks made you feel.

Personal injury

It is the *pattern* of incidents which reveals *intent*. If you or a colleague have highlighted the danger posed by the bully's behaviour, and the employer has chosen to take no action, then if you continue to suffer detriment the employer may be guilty of negligence. Make contact with as many predecessors as possible and get written statements about the bully's behaviour, to obtain information and insight into the psychiatric injury caused by the bullying.

To pursue a personal injury case you will at present almost certainly need a diagnosis of post-traumatic stress disorder (PTSD) from a specialist or consultant. Note that in the wake of Sheriff v Klyne Tugs (Lowestoft) Ltd, personal injury arising from bullying, harassment and discrimination must now be handled at the Employment Tribunal.

Defamation of character

The bully's inaccurate and vindictive assessments of their target could form the basis of legal action for defamation of character. The employer's claim that you are suffering a mental illness when you are psychiatrically injured might also constitute defamation of character.

Libel (written) and slander (spoken)

Written defamation or spoken abuse, sent or hurled on a regular basis, constitutes bullying, and may be breaking the slander or libel laws and may therefore provide satisfaction in the courts. This is a very expensive procedure.

Malicious Communications Act 1988

Section 1 provides for the offence of sending letters, etc. (including e-mails, known as 'flaming'), with intent to cause distress or anxiety. It refers to communications that convey grossly offensive or indecent messages, threats or information that is false and known by the sender to be such (e.g. false accusations about the recipient). Any person knowing or who should know that they will or are likely to cause offence is guilty of an offence under this Act. This behaviour also appears to fall under The Prevention of Harassment Act 1977.

Harassing and abusive phone calls constitute bullying behaviour and can be dealt with under The Prevention of Harassment Act 1977 or section 43 of The Telecommunications Act 1984, under which they may constitute a criminal offence.

Corporate manslaughter

Where a person commits suicide as a result of being bullied, and the employer knew of the bullying but chose to take no action, a charge of corporate manslaughter may be brought. Under The Health and Safety at Work Act 1974 section 2, it may be possible to bring a case of corporate manslaughter, provided the bullying or harassment was reported and posed a reasonable risk of psychiatric injury and even if that was not the direct (no causal link) cause of death.

Unlike gross negligence under common law, where a causal link must be established (that is the negligence was a substantial cause of the death), no such link has to be established under section 2 of the Health and Safety Act. What this means is that even if an employer was not directly involved (non-causal) in bullying an employee (causal), they may be liable if they knew or ought to have known that the employee was being bullied and that employee committed suicide because of the bullying.

Contempt of court

Once Industrial Tribunal proceedings have been started, any attempt by the bully or the employer to warn off witnesses (e.g. intimidating other employees into retracting statements by threatening them with loss of job) could be seen as a contempt of court. If this happens, inform the Tribunal in writing at once.

Common assault

In the UK in March 1997 a 16-year-old girl was convicted of common assault for bullying, which was all verbal with little or no physical contact. This case sets a precedent in UK law that assault can be psychological as well as physical. You will need to report the bullying to the police quickly. The police may not be interested, but persist.

Human Rights Act 1998

The following could be seen as a breach of the European Convention on Human Rights, which has now been accepted by the UK:

■ denial of representation, e.g. when attending a disciplinary hearing

■ denial of the right to seek justice by using the regulations to prevent a case from being presented at Tribunal

■ insistence on signing a gagging clause: linking settlement to signing the gagging clause could be seen as blackmail.

Statutory Instruments

If you're a UK public sector employee you may be able to make use of Statutory Instrument No. 1680 Local Government (Discretionary Payments) Regulations 1996 to get your pension increased to 85% of normal earnings. In certain cases this Statutory Instrument can be used in instances of early retirement on grounds of ill health.

But beware: I know of one case where a Civil Service department tried to use this to stop a person who was suffering extreme ill-health through bullying from fighting her case against her employer. The offer (which amounted to blackmail) was that if she dropped her case the employer would ensure that she received early retirement and full pension rights immediately. She wisely refused and as I write is going ahead with her fight.

Academic statutes

Under university statutes a lecturer has the right of appeal against unfair dismissal. The statutes are derived from the model statutes in the 1988 Education Reform Act. The advantage of this course of action is that unlike unfair dismissal at an employment tribunal it is not subject to a compensation ceiling, thus the statutes generally give academics more rights than they have under the Employment Rights Act. For example, universities are required in all cases to apply the principles of justice and fairness, there are specific procedures that they are required to follow, and there is a guarantee that people will not be dismissed or placed under threat of dismissal for their opinions. The university has to appoint (and pay) a QC to hear the appeal, on top of their own lawyers.

European law specific to bullying

Sweden is the only country in Europe with legislation specific to bullying. Victimisation at work is covered by an Ordinance of the Swedish National Board of Occupational Safety and Health containing Provisions on measures against Victimisation at Work (adopted 21 September 1993).

To conclude, I believe that I have demonstrated that, with a little research and effort, legal protection (in the absence of specific law) in current UK law is available to obtain satisfaction for being bullied at work. It is essential, however, to obtain proper competent legal representation before you do battle.

Quick reference guide 17

Case law relevant to bullying and harassment

Bullying and personal injury

➡ *Walford v Ford Motor Company (1998)*

Bullying and stress

➡ *Lancaster v Birmingham City Council (1999)*

➡ *Noonan v Liverpool City Council (1999)*

Bullying and post-traumatic stress disorder

➡ *Messenger v Oxfordshire County Council (1998)*

Bullying and harassment

➡ *Go Kidz Go v Bourdouane (EAT 10 September 1996)*

➡ *Phelan v Pizza Express plc*

➡ *Kramer v UNISON (1998)*

➡ *Gilbert v Midland Bank (1998)*

➡ *Stubbs v Lincolnshire Police*

Chapter 6

Stress and the workplace

So, if you are to fight back effectively good stress management is essential to help you stay negative stress free. Knowing what stress is and recognising the symptoms is a good place to start.

We all hear, and may even talk, regularly about stress. In a lot of cases stress is simply applied to the way we feel after a particularly difficult day. 'How are you?' 'I'm stressed out' is probably one of the most often posed questions and answers used today, and while this response may very well be dictated by the way that person is feeling at the time, it would be wrong to diagnose that person as suffering from a stress-related illness.

Most people suffer stress. A lot of people need stress to function better (i.e. 'positive stress', more about this later), whereas some people are 'drained' on a regular basis by stressful situations but recover naturally and carry on. For others, however, stress becomes something they cannot shake off and they deteriorate into suffering full-blown stress-related illnesses. What I intend to give you here are some tools to help you manage your stress levels effectively.

Quick reference guide 18

Symptoms of stress

➡ Excessive and sudden hair loss

➡ Mouth ulcers

➡ Cold sores

➡ Chest pains

➡ High blood pressure

➡ Disruptions in heart rhythm (palpitations, etc.)

➡ Disturbed sleep patterns

➡ Loss of libido (in both men and women)

➡ An appearance or reappearance of psoriasis or eczema

➡ Muscle tension, leading to neck ache, shoulder ache, twitches, etc.

➡ Gastritis

➡ Irritable bowel syndrome

➡ Aggravation of asthma

➡ Undue anxiety

➡ Loss of concentration

➡ Memory losses

➡ Depression

➡ Mood swings

➡ Loss of appetite

➡ Bingeing

➡ Amenorrhoea (no periods)

➡ Sleeping too much

➡ Seeming to catch every cold or bug that's around

All the above symptoms can be ailments in their own right but can be caused or exacerbated by higher stress levels than someone can cope with. If you suffer any of the above regularly don't hesitate to contact your doctor.

Behaviour

When we are stressed our behaviour changes and it manifests itself in different ways according to our personality. Some people take everything in their stride, shrugging off the pressure or even welcoming pressure and using it to help them achieve more. This kind of behaviour is applicable to those who 'thrive' on the day-to-day stressors that appear to affect others in a much more negative way. The latter are the people who are more likely to suffer ill-health because of stress. For example, they may:

- suffer anxiety
- become irritable
- show aggression
- become prone to mood swings
- suffer complete withdrawal.

These signs may often be indicators that someone is starting to suffer clinically from a stress-related illness. There are hundreds of reasons why this may happen to someone in the workplace and here are a few examples:

- bullying
- harassment
- unfair workload
- their role at work
- their relationships at work
- lack of career development
- culture change.

As I mentioned earlier, some of these would only serve to galvanise certain people into action but others would find them impossible to cope with.

Quick reference guide 19

Behavioural indicators that stress may be affecting you

➡ Lethargy sets in

➡ You are starting to use alcohol or drugs to unwind

➡ You begin needing more sleep

➡ You snack more than you eat proper meals

➡ You no longer discuss, you argue

➡ You become paranoid

➡ You become weepy for no reason

➡ You begin to prefer your own company to the company of others

➡ Your temper always seems to be simmering under the surface

➡ You are often angry with yourself

➡ You are often angry with your family, even the cat!

➡ You take up smoking or smoke more

➡ You stop exercising

➡ One minute you're happy, the next you're sad

Positive stress

It is generally accepted that we all need a certain amount of 'stress' to push us on and inspire us. This is often referred to as 'positive stress'. As long ago as the first century AD, the Greek philosopher Epictetus said: 'Man is not affected by events but his perception of them.' A way of putting that in relation to stress is: 'It is not the event that causes stress, it is your perception of the event that causes it'. For each individual, that which pushes them over the edge will be different, as will that which creates drive and ambition. It is obvious that some of us thrive on pressure while others don't, I'm sure we have all had work colleagues who never seem to be fazed by the amount of work thrust upon them, who always seem to take the last-minute rush in their stride and never complain about targets, no matter how difficult to achieve they may seem to the rest of us.

As long as we think of stress as a negative force, we will strive to keep it at bay, ensuring we don't have stress in the first place. In truth, stress is an energy force within all of us and is an ingredient needed to achieve our optimum performance. Positive stress is beneficial and is essential in helping us achieve our goals and stimulate vitality.

Embracing stress as a positive force and channelling our thoughts and feelings in a positive direction will help us to fight back, against the bully, the harasser, being overworked, being undermined, etc.

Think about stress in the way you think about oil pressure in a car. High oil pressure or low oil pressure can be problematic, but you never want the oil pressure to disappear completely. It is the same with stress: when not regulated or controlled or ignored, stress can be harmful to your health; too little stress can lead to apathy, tiredness and illness. A major step towards successful stress management is to find and maintain a balance that works for you at each stage of your life.

When you are being bullied and you are feeling battered, it's only natural to start falling into the negative stress trap. It is essential that you look for the positive in what's happening around you; it is essential that you start to fight back. Begin an exercise regime, take time out for yourself, work on strategies to combat the bully. There is much sound and well-proven advice in this book for you to work with.

The stress graph in Figure 6.1 should give you an idea of where your negative stress is likely to kick in. By using the knowledge you have of your own abilities and optimum level of effectiveness you should be able to keep negative stress at bay.

So, is stress a good or a bad thing? I believe that some stress is good for us, especially those of us who enjoy a bit of pressure or even need it to help our motivation. But if our self-worth is persistently attacked and self-doubt appears we can succumb very quickly to the negative stress influence.

I think that awareness is probably the key here. We all need to be vigilant to the pressures of the workplace and particularly to the pressures that managers and some colleagues may put upon us. While accepting that stress is not just a work-related problem, it is worth remembering that one-third of our day is spent at work and any problems in the workplace can exacerbate pressure and problems from elsewhere. Conversely, undue pressure, bullying, harassment, etc., can cause problems at home.

To me it is still the most terrifying thought that good, honest, hardworking people can be brought to their knees, and even to the brink of suicide and beyond, by selfish, uncaring, manipulative emotional cripples, whose only aim in life appears to be to destroy the lives of others by bullying them into the ground.

I firmly believe in good stress management, taking exercise, sleeping and eating regularly, good time management and fighting back by becoming more assertive. But by far and away one of the best stress busters is talking to someone. Get it off your chest to someone you trust, someone who you know is not judge-

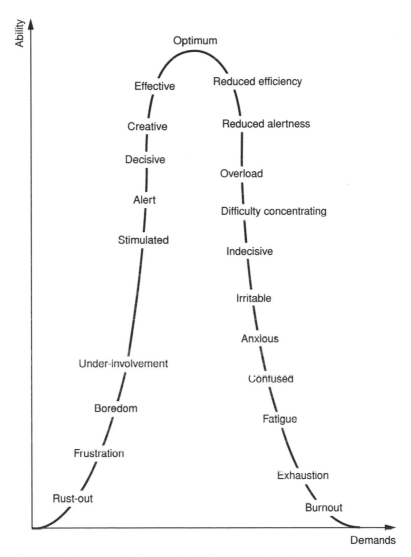

Figure 6.1 Stress graph. Source: Andy Ellis, workplacebullying.co.uk

mental and who cares for you. If this is not possible speak to your doctor and ask their advice. It may even be possible to attend some counselling sessions, but just telling someone what is happening to you will be a great relief and will go a long way

Quick reference guide 20

Positive stress words

➡ Passion

➡ Motivation

➡ Excitement

➡ Desire

➡ Ambition

➡ Belief

➡ Optimism

➡ Hope

➡ Empowerment

Quick reference guide 21

Stress busters

➡ Learn to say 'no' to some demands and to delegate tasks

➡ Smile inwardly when someone is nasty to you. Think of their unacceptable behaviour as their problem, not yours

➡ Treat yourself regularly: go to the theatre, the movies or a yoga class, or have a massage

➡ Make time each day to switch off with family and friends

➡ Always have some special goal to achieve, e.g. a romantic weekend or holiday

➡ One evening a week go out, enjoy yourself, instead of slumping in front of the TV

➡ Go to bed by midnight as often as you can

➡ Don't oversleep: keeping regular hours preserves energy levels

➡ From time to time pack the children off for a few hours and put time aside for yourself

➡ Wear colours that reflect your mood: bright oranges or yellows are energising; white, purple and green are calming

➡ Watch your diet

➡ By all means, have a relaxing drink, but drink equal measures of water

➡ Change your negative thoughts to positive thoughts. Think of a terrific holiday you have had and relive it

➡ Take full responsibility for how you feel rather than blaming other people. Don't say, 'You are annoying me' say, 'I feel annoyed when you repeatedly ask me to help you catch up on your work'

➡ Be positive: imagine that your glass is half full, not half empty

Quick reference guide 22

More stress busters

➡ Work off your stress with physical activity

➡ Talk to someone you really trust

➡ Learn to accept what you cannot change

➡ Avoid self-medication through alcohol, nicotine, tranquillisers, etc.

➡ Take time out to play

➡ Get enough sleep

➡ Deal with one problem at a time

➡ Manage your time better

➡ If you are ill don't carry on as if you're not

➡ Learn to say 'no!' more often

➡ Delegate some responsibilities

➡ Be realistic and honest about your abilities

➡ Know when you are tired and do something about it

➡ Learn relaxation exercises and do them

➡ Become more and 'be' assertive

towards helping you to overcoming the problem. It is generally accepted that recognising that you are suffering negative stress and may be suffering ill-health because of it is 90% of the battle won.

Finally, there is only one person who can overcome stress-related problems and that is you. You and only you can decide not to be bullied or harassed any more. You and only you can say 'no!' and do something about it.

There are several things that I cannot emphasise often enough: you must talk to somebody if you feel you are being targeted, you must be assertive in your dealings with people, you must fight back and you must seek out good advice from people who are trained in dealing with the problem. Finally, if you have been put in a position where you have no support or redress, leaving the situation that you find untenable and seeking work elsewhere is not the action of a loser, it is the action of a winner: someone who has fought back, made good sound, positive, forward-thinking judgements and left the losers behind.

The last case history is not personal to me, it is a well-known landmark case. I have chosen it because it is inspiring in the sense that the woman who was bullied in the most vicious manner fought back and won.

It was Aesop in the fable The Wolf and the Lamb who said: 'Any excuse will serve a tyrant'. Ensure that your guard doesn't drop and your behaviour is such that the tyrant leaves you well alone.

Case history 4 (Tanya Clayton)

An Industrial Tribunal has made a record award of £200,000 to a woman who suffered bullying and abuse over the five years she worked for the Hereford and Worcester Fire Brigade. The award was made against the Brigade and two sub-officers were sued personally.

Tanya Clayton joined the Brigade in 1989, following five years in the army, and was subjected to a catalogue of abuse. She was notified of her retirement from the Brigade on health grounds in a letter dated 26 July 1994, the day before her complaint to an Industrial Tribunal of bullying and victimisation, on the grounds of sex discrimination, was to be heard. The original tribunal heard that a senior Brigade officer introduced her to new colleagues by saying 'the good news is you are getting another member of the watch, the bad news is that the new member of the watch is a woman – Tanya Clayton'. She was also referred to as 'a stupid f****** cow' and a 'tart'.

Harsh regime

The tribunal found that she was subjected to a 'harsh and unfriendly regime', unlike her male colleagues who were treated well. On one occasion she was spun around for an hour on a turntable ladder one-hundred feet above the ground because it was assumed she was afraid of heights. She was also forced to make tea for the men and serve it to them in their beds at the station.

Unanimous decision

The treatment cost Tanya her career and her marriage. She moved out of the area to be near her parents.

After a hearing which lasted a total of 23 days over several months the tribunal unanimously upheld her complaints. Hereford and Worcester County Council appealed to the Employment Appeal Tribunal. The EAT unanimously rejected the entire appeal, with Lord Justice Mummery commenting that one of the grounds of appeal put forward was 'an abuse of the whole appeal process'. The case was sent back to the Industrial Tribunal at Shrewsbury to assess compensation.

Apology

The award represents compensation for injury to feelings, future loss of earnings and loss of pension. She has since received a full apology from Hereford and Worcester County Council for the appalling treatment she suffered.

Tanya Clayton said: 'I am glad that, at long last, this is all over. I entered the Fire Brigade with high hopes and ambition, I left it a shadow of my former self. My thoughts are with those who continue to suffer bullying in their workplaces. I hope that this award, which will help me to begin to rebuild my life, will cause employers to look closely at what is happening in their workplaces'.

Message to employers

John Gordon, regional officer of the Fire Brigades Union which backed the case, said: 'This is a victory tinged with sadness. Tanya's life has been devastated. The message from the FBU to employers is that this kind of despicable behaviour will not be tolerated and must be stopped'.

Janet Smith of Thompsons Solicitors, who acted for the FBU, said: 'Tanya's treatment was extreme and is reflected in the size of the award. The message to employers is loud and clear: bullying is not only very unpleasant, it can also be very expensive.'

Chapter 7

Quotes from people who inspire

If you are going through hell, keep going.

Sir Winston Churchill

- Never tolerate bullying behaviour.
- Don't just give people a chance to speak – let them know they are being heard.
- Nix the 'Don't bring me problems, bring me solutions' mentality.
- Everyone speaks three languages – that of speech, that of silence and that of the body.
- Teach people about the business, so that they can fall in love with it.

Robbie Stamp, CEO, TVD Inc.

Nowadays society is evil. It finds subtle ways of torture, to destroy the life-quick, to get at the life-quick in a man in every possible form. And still a man can hold out, if he can laugh and listen to the Holy Ghost.

Edgar Allan Poe

I was an attractive boy, and it was the norm for any boy considered a pretty boy to be wolf-whistled at. They'd sit on their window ledges above, whistling and shouting 'tart, tart'. Such remorseless nastiness squeezed every last trace of self-confidence from me. At one point, I stood on Windsor Bridge and contemplated throwing myself off.

> Taken from: *The Observer*, 4 November 2001
> Sir Ranulph Fiennes, polar explorer, bullied at Eton

I became shy because I was overweight. At 16 I was 13 st and was called 'Blubber'. It was pathetic and childish, but girls are so catty. It lasted for about two years. Eventually, I must have told my mother, and she took it up with the masters. They dealt with the situation without exposing my identity. I think that's very important today in cases of bullying.

Kate Winslet, tormented at school because of her weight

There was this boy who we used to call the cock of the school, who'd boss everyone around and push in front of the queue. The abuse was stuff like, 'Hey, nigger! I'm talking to you, blacky'. Guys would call me things like 'coon' and 'golliwog'. In those days, golliwogs were on the jam jars and we black kids hated them.

> **Tessa Sanderson, Olympic champion javelin-thrower, subjected to racial abuse throughout her school life**

The fact that I was born in Wales may have played a part. My tormentors were a clannish group. I didn't tell my family. For some reason, I felt ashamed that it should be happening to me. It lasted only a term. I developed a dreadful stammer, which alerted my parents.

> **Martyn Lewis, terrible term at school in Northern Ireland**

Anyone can be a target for the bully. While it's easy and natural to think that it's never happened to anyone else, these are some memories of people who were bullied and how it affected them.

The following quotes are taken from schoolzone.co.uk

One teacher was the most cruel man. He used to call me names in front of the other kids, called me 'girlie' and 'lassie'. It went on and on for four years and I hated him.

Boy George, singer

Bullies are just dumping all their own unhappiness on to somebody else.

Jeremy Hardy, comedian

I think it's so valuable in those circumstances to have parents who will get involved. If my parents hadn't been interested, it would have been even worse.

Jo Brand, comedian

I was the absolutely natural target for bullying. I was interested in flowers and animals and was very warm and sought warmth, which were not particularly helpful characteristics for settling down with a bunch of tiny thugs. I kept trying to think of all the ways in which I could commit suicide. It was a measure of my despair and unhappiness. It has given me a life-long aversion to bullies. I actually see it as a responsibility to take them on face to face.

Sir John Harvey Jones, industrialist

I don't think bullies remember who they bullied. It's the bullied who remember who the bullies were.

Sir Ranulph Fiennes, explorer

The ironic thing about bullying is that the child who is getting bullied needs the immediate help, but the source of the pain (the bully) is in more need in the long term because they've got large psychological or social problems that need addressing.

Duncan Goodhew, Olympic gold medallist

I used to try and steel myself but it didn't stop the fact that I used to get jumped on regularly and had to fight back all the time.

Sir Cliff Richard, entertainer

Companies should realize that the only real assets they have are their people, unfortunately, many large British organizations have lost sight of this Holy Grail.

Sir Richard Branson

My personal favourite is a quote from one of the wisest men ever to walk upon our planet, Mahatma Gandhi, who said:

When I despair, I remember that all through history the way of truth and love has always won. There have been tyrants and murderers and for a time they seem invincible but in the end, they always fall – think of it, ALWAYS.

While most of these quotes refer to people's schooldays and the reasons for the bullying are often quite different to those of the workplace, the targets still remember it. Once bullied you never forget, but the other side of the coin is that once you have beaten the bully you never forget you can.

The knowledge gained from reading this book should stand you in good stead for fighting back against the bully. It should be a reminder for constant vigilance, it will help you to formulate your plan for fighting back, and you should use it as a toolbox to enable you to fix the problem.

Useful reading and websites

Websites dealing with workplace bullying

www.successunlimited.co.uk
www.workplacebullying.co.uk
www.bullybusters.org
www.workdoctor.com
www.worktrauma.org
www.workplace-bullying-books.co.uk
www.bullydissolver.com
www.andreaadamstrust.org
www.suzylamplugh.org
www.schoolzone.co.uk

Books dealing with workplace bullying and assertiveness

Field, T. *Bully in Sight*, Success Unlimited, 1996.
Wheatley, R. *Bullying at Work*, Hodder & Stoughton, 1999.
Raynor, C., Hoel, H., Cooper, C. *Workplace Bullying*, Taylor & Francis, 2001.
Back, K., Back, K. *Assertiveness at Work*, McGraw-Hill, 1999.
Eggert, M.A. *The Assertive Pocketbook*, Management Pocketbooks, 1997.

Employment law websites

www.freelawyer.co.uk
www.legalshop.co.uk
www.thompsons.law.co.uk
www.emplaw.co.uk
www.employmentlaw.co.uk
www.tiger.gov.uk

Index

Other self-help books from McGraw-Hill

How to Get a Job You'll Love – A practical guide to unlocking your talents and finding your ideal career By LEES
Price: £14.99
ISBN: 0077098005
A unique and creative look at career planning. It takes one step back and teaches you how to think outside the box, tap into your hidden talents and identify what type of career you really want.

Living with Fear By MARKS
Price: £14.99
ISBN: 0077097580
Living with Fear is a self-help book that gives practical advice to people who are suffering from phobias, panic, obsessions, rituals or traumatic distress.

Manager's Guide to Self-Development By PEDLER ET AL
Price: £19.99
ISBN: 0077098307
This book is designed as a self-development programme for managers seeking to develop skills such as mental agility, creativity, social skills and emotional resilience.

Assertiveness at Work – A practical guide to handling awkward situations By BACK AND BACK
Price: £14.99
ISBN: 0077095332
Over 100,000 copies sold worldwide. This book is a practical guide for developing your own natural assertiveness to benefit both yourself and your organisation.

Time Management 24/7 – How to double your effectiveness By PHILLIPS (forthcoming)
Price: £9.99
ISBN: 007709963X
Traditional time management techniques are no longer sufficient in our 24/7 economy. In offering advice on how to identify and focus on your priorities in life, change your behaviour and get the most out of electronic tools, this book shows you how to lead a more balanced life.

Walking Tall – Key steps to total image impact By EVERETT (forthcoming)
Price: £10.99
ISBN: 0077099672
Walking Tall is an empowering collection of trade secrets, which will ensure your personal image keeps you one step ahead in the game and a cut above the rest.

Open for Business – How to write letters that get results By FERGSUON
Price: £19.99
ISBN: 0077097696
The book aims to encourage readers to become more confident, effective writers. It looks at how to get started, how to overcome writer's block, how to write a five-minute outline, how to build up a rapport, how to promise and deliver benefits, and how to get a 'yes' result.

The Great Escape – Your guide to early retirement and financial freedom By WHITE
Price: £14.99
ISBN: 0077098412
The Great Escape is an accessible guide to planning early retirement.

Stepping Up – A woman's guide to career development By KAZEROUNIAN
Price: £19.99
ISBN: 0077098021
Based on interviews with women across Europe, this practical guide aims to help women overcome everyday challenges and develop their careers.

When Life Gives You Lemons: Remarkable Stories of People Overcoming Adversity By TRESNIOWSKI
Price: £12.99,
ISBN: 007135591X
Rich in wisdom, hope, and intimate portraits of real people, this is a book which manages to capture the essence of courage, delivering a set of priceless lessons readers can immediately incorporate into their own lives. Alex Tresniowski relates 21

inspiring experiences of ordinary folks and then shows exactly how anyone can make the most of the vast stores of strength residing within us all.

Addicted To Unhappiness By HEINEMAN PIEPER
Price: £ 16.99,
ISBN: 0071385495
The powerful new book by the bestselling author team of Martha and William Pieper, is based on the Piepers' discovery that the most common obstacle to fulfillment is a secret addiction to unhappiness.

How to Deal With Emotionally Explosive People By BERNSTEIN
Price: £ 10.99,
ISBN: 007138569X
A valuable source of insight and guidance on how to deal effectively with the 'walking time bombs' in our midst.

Why We Hate By DOZIER
Price: £ 18.99,
ISBN: 0809224836
Why We Hate presents readers with a comprehensive nine-step strategy for controlling and eliminating hate.

Crucial Conversations – Tools for Talking When the Stakes Are High By PATTERSON
Price: £ 10.99,
ISBN: 0071401946
Crucial Conversations offers readers a proven seven-point strategy for achieving their goals in all those emotionally, psychologically, or legally charged situations that can arise in their professional and personal lives.

Emotional Vampires: Dealing with People who Drain you Dry By ALBERT J. BERNSTEIN
Price: £ 9.99,
ISBN: 0071381678
The best-selling author of Dinosaur Brains offers protection from people who seek to destroy the emotional and psychological well-being of others.

The Disease to Please – Curing the People-Pleasing Syndrome By BRAIKER
Price: £ 10.99,
ISBN: 0071385649
The Disease to Please explodes the dangerous myth that 'people pleasing' is a benign problem. It is the first book to treat people pleasing as a serious psychological syndrome, and it breaks new ground in its approach to offer a cure.

If you wish to order any of the above books then please contact our Customer Services Department on Tel: +44 (0) 1628 502700 Fax: +44 (0) 1628 635895